A LIFE LONG ROMANCE

A Life Long Romance
With Nature and the Wild

VIJAY VERMA

GenNext Publication

ISBN : 978-93-8022-249-3
Price : ₹ 630

First Published in 2016

Published by

GenNext Publication
5, Ansari Road, Darya Ganj
New Delhi-110002
Ph. : 23282060, 23261060
Fax : 011-23285914
E-mail: gennext@hotmail.com

Printed at : G Print Process, Delhi

Cataloging in Publication Data—DK
Courtesy: D.K. Agencies (P) Ltd. <docinfo@dkagencies.com>

Verma, Vijay, author.
A life long romance : with nature and the wild/ Vijay Verma.
pages cm
ISBN 9789380222493

1. Verma, Vijay. 2. Hunting—India—Anecdotes. 3. India. Army—Officers—Biography. 4. Wildlife art. I. Title

DDC 799.2954 23

Dedication

This book on wildlife memoirs and sketches is dedicated to Haider Mian, Matroo (gond tribal), Topo, Choti and Karna (Baiga tribals), great natural born experts on jungle lore and wildlife, who helped in the chase and who conveyed so much knowledge and pleasure; and to Indu (my late wife) who always stood by me in all my endeavors, Arun (my younger son) who in his positive and persuasive style, made me put this work together and Arjun (the elder son) who has been a staunch conservationalist.

Special Thanks

A special thanks to Sally, my dear friend, who helped in the final shape of the book and choosing of the tittle. And also my elder sister Kamla, who always encouraged me in this endeavour.

Contents

List of Color Photo 11
Introduction 15
Preface 19
Foreword 21

1. **Romance with Wild Life and Forest and Real Vintage Stories** **23**

2. **Espirit-de-corps** **29**

3. **Vengeance will be mine!** **35**

4. **NAWAB** **43**
(Jabalpur 1942-43)

5. **The Cobra in the Pee Pot!** **51**
(Katni 1944)

6. **The Man Eating Leopard of Jhilpa** **55**
(Near Nagpur 1942-43)

7. **Haidar Mian–The Forest Wizard** **69**
(Kolash, Nanded 1950-51)

8. **Survival of the Fittest** **77**
(Nagaland and MP 1958-59)

9. **Bilaspur Days** **81**
(Bilaspur, MP 1959-60)

10. **A Tiger in the Mines** **89**
(Baitul, MP 1959)

11. The Leopard in the Storm **93**
(Baitul, MP 1960)

12. The Honeymoon Tiger **97**
(Sarguja, MP 1964)

13. Elephants, Elephants Everywhere **113**
(Dehradun, UK 1964)

14. The Ones That Got Away And Some That Did Not **119**
(Dehradun, 1963-72)

15. Outings in the Shiwaliks and Khadar of Ghaghra River **131**
(Dehradun, 1963-64 &1975-76)

16. Wildlife! On the Pakistan Border **137**
(Alhar, 1965)

17. The Brow Antlered Deer **143**
(Lungleh, Mizoram 1966-67)

18. The Dhol/Sone Kutta – The Wild Dog of India **147**
(Mandla, MP)

19. The Rajasthan Experience **151**
(Jaisalmer, Rajasthan 1981-84)

20. The Bird Sanctuary of Bharatpur **155**
(Rajasthan, 1989-94)

21. The Boar which had Nine Lives **165**
(Dehradun, 1999-2000)

22. Some Thoughts on Wildlife Protection **173**

23. Some Suggestions for Protection of the Tiger **177**

Jungle Sketch Book and Vintage Photographs 183

24. Khatawli **195**

List of Color Photo

Fig. 1 : Tiger stalking his prey a Sambhar Stag.

Fig. 2 : Tiger Killing the Sambhar Stag.

Fig. 3 : Tiger eating its kill.

Fig. 4 : Tiger walking past the Sambhar herd after having fed on its kill. The deer are not afraid of him as they know that he has just eaten his prey and will not kill again for a few days.

Fig. 5 : A Peacock calling from a tree before Roasting down for the night.

Fig. 6 : The cattle lifter of Kinor- is on his kill-buffalo killed by him.

Fig. 7 : One of the tigers rear broken leg is but he is charging my father who can be seen-shooting him.

Fig. 8 : The cattle lifter of Kinor being carried to the car when enroute another tiger was seen.

Fig. 9 : The tigeress was wounded in the jaw therefore could not bite Maj Gehlot, who is pinned down by her Maj Gill is Seen loading his weapon before finally shooting the wounded tigress.

Fig. 10 : The buffalo hiding behind the spaces of creeps before attaching the hunter

Fig. 11 : The buffloe (Kana) sitting among the bull rushes

Fig. 12 : The buffaloe getting out of the pond and heading for the forest when it was shot and wounded.

Fig. 13 : The buffloe going and killing the hunter, the tracker can be seen having climbed a true to save himself.

Fig. 14 : Difference between African buffloe and a Indian buffaloe
Fig. 15 : Cobra can he seen in the pee-pot

"Subhan Teri Kudrat" !!

("Oh ! Almighty What a Land of Natural Beauty you have Created")

Babur *the great – The First Mughal Emperor of* India, (date AD 1526).

According to legend, greatly impressed by the wild and natural beauty of Hindustan, said these words in great praise, while crossing the planes and forest lands of North India, on first *hearing the call of the* ***Black Partridge.***

Introduction

The idea of this book has been with me since I was ten years old in 1947; when I actually saw and met my childhood hero, Jim Corbett at the Nainital bus stop. The other great man who helped to make my resolve firm was, "A sparrow falls", Salim Ali; whom I was fortunate to meet at the US Club in Colaba, Bombay, in 1984. He took me aside to ask me in great detail about the Himalayan quail, which I had mentioned to him, having seen the bird behind the *Sher-ka-danda*, near our school in Nainital. This bird is now extinct and was last seen around the time and location I had mentioned. My personal hobbies and likings seem to match these two personalities in intensity for the love of the wild. As I enjoyed roaming in the jungles around the school (Nainital) looking for pheasants, collecting wild bird eggs, seeking out the otters near our Narsinghpur home in a stream, and hunting with the catapult, in "Early Days".

Accompanying father as a young boy, observing the leopards around Jhilpa was an amazing and thrilling experience as also the machan in the orange orchard from which the "Man eater of Jhilpa" was shot by my father in 1944.

I had a God given talent in my hand of sketching and drawing. As is said a drawing speaks a thousand words'; the racket tailed drongo or the mighty tiger, the tiger attacking a boar and the water birds of Bharatpur bird sanctuary, the sambhar stag sitting in a mud bath and so on. Discovering the big pugmarks of a huge tiger around the car in which we slept all night (myself age eight years and my brother ten years). See jungle sketch book.

The book is based on a lifetime of anecdotes and memoirs of encounters with wildlife, birds and animals. The thrills of tracking and finally sighting a huge sambhar after following it for 15 miles over trackless terrain "Bilaspur Days".

On getting married in 1964, visit to Sarguja (Ambikapur) in M.P. See "the honeymoon tiger", planning, tying up baits in the block and despite the last minute hic-cups of a gun going off by mistake just before the beat *(hanka)* was to start, a comedy of errors, finally success.

An Army career of 32 plus years in the elite Rajput Regiment (Infantry), I trekked over possibly every hilltop and Valley along the border! (especially in the east, Naga hills and Mizoram). Starting from Nagaland "Survival of the fittest" where I saw one of the biggest snakes. An enormous Python in a nullah. Lungleh in Mizoram, was an eye opener in the varied wild life, including the *thamin* or brow antlered deer. "Wildlife on the Pakistan Border" had a spice of its own. Some great and thrilling experiences, going after the blue sheep *(bharal)* on the Indo-Tibbetan border, the narrow escape from falling down a *khudd* to certain disaster while chasing it! The elusive *thar,* the golden fleece goat of India, in the *Maral Kanda* high altitude block in Himachal Pradesh, in "some that got away and some that did not".

The unique experience of tracking elephants in Barkot block near Rishikesh (Dehradun), on a special permit from the local administration in 1964, see "*Elephants Elephants everywhere".

At Bharatpur, I was lucky to befriend a fine young forest officer, the then director of the bird sanctuary (1992-97)

A.S. Brar (now chief conservator of forest in the IFS Rajasthan cadre); due to his positive and courageous actions, in spite of political lobby's interference in his job, the sanctuary revived and was at its best during his tenure and some years later. "See the bird sanctuary of Bharatpur.

The wild boar is a brave and big hearted animal found in all our jungles and shrub land. They also develop an uncanny sixth sense due to which they have survived so far! *The boar which had nine lives.

There are some 50 'sketches of wild birds and animals and one or two of humans! *Hyder Mian,* my favourite, an ex-forest guard at **Hyder Mian* the forest wizard of Kaulash; a perfect wild game warden he would have made. Jungle people like *Hyder, Topo, Karna, Matru ...* possessed awesome talent in jungle lore and a love for the jungle fauna, it is these types of people around our main tiger reserves, who should have a "big say" in the scheme of things to protect the tiger see *Some suggestions for improving the existing organisation for protection of tigers in the tiger reserves.

You may find this unusual collection, interesting; sketches, writings and vintage pictures covering a period from 1934 to 1965, to date a collection of a lifetime of some unique experiences and interesting episodes and memoirs.

Vijay Verma

Fig. 1 : Tiger stalking his paw a Sambhar Stag.

Preface

The natural and the wild world is beautiful if left undisturbed and tranquil. But we humans have disturbed the calm tranquillity of nature to such an extent that it seems impossible to get things back to what they were once.

But there is a contradiction in the way we perceive nature and the wild, where non-violence as we humans understand it, does not exist. Non-violence is basically a human, concept and brain child. Kill or be killed, tooth and claw, blood and gore are, and always have been a prelude to peace and tranquillity in the wilderness.

The above is so well brought home to a nature lover in the deep forests where the mighty **Tiger** rules; when he hears the alarm call of a sambhar, honk — *tonk! - fee - tumm* — !, just prior to being overpowered and killed by him. It is late afternoon, but soon after this violent outburst of the sambhar kill being made by the **Tiger**, yes the King is having his supper after a break of seven may be ten days when he had his last belly full of wild boar. He will now kill only after another seven may be ten or may be more days. This law of the jungle is understood and accepted by the herds of sambhar, cheetal, wild boar, who all know that the king will not kill again for sometime! This is the time of peace and tranquillity for them. All is peaceful as the peafowl-flies on to the tall silk cotton tree (*sehmal*) branches, *sellette* against the dying sun and give his *meeaoo* ! *meeaoo!* Call, just before dark, the night jars start there *chuk-chukka-chuk,* and fly low over the forest tracks showing off their night-vision site. The grazing deer, see the tiger walking, gliding bye silently, his belly full and after having had a drink of water at the nearby pool. Although he is passing bye quite close from them, they by and large ignore him; no alarm calls, and go back to there grazing and nibbling, which they have to do all the time, day in and day out. Yes, a vegetarian, herbivourous big animal, has to eat almost all the time, day and night, to meet their basic, minimum requirement of grass and foliage, to stay active and alive; whereas a **Tiger** will eat once in ten days. Yes, so, in the jungle code, this is the cycle of violence and non-violence, in the deep jungles, where **TIGER** is king!!

Fig. 2 : Tiger Killing the Sambhar Stag.

Fig. 3 : Tiger eating its kill.

Fig. 4 : Tiger walking past the Sambhar herd after having fed on its kill. The deer are not afraid of him as they know that he has just eaten his prey and will not kill again for a few days.

Fig. 5 : A Peacock calling from a tree before soroting down for the night.

Foreword

A distinguished Army Officer, Col. (Retd.) Vijay Verma, whom I taught during his boyhood days at Birla Vidyamandir, Nainital (formerly Philandar Smith College), was strikingly different from most boys. Though a little quiet but perceptive, Vijay had an unusual longing for the jungle and took keen interest in adventure, games and sports. It was not surprising that his father, an IAS officer, sent him to a Residential Public School nestled in the lushgreen wooded hills of Nainital in order to grow and flourish in an ideal environment.

The quality of a narrative is largely dependent on the author's sensitivity, passion and lucidity with which he shares his experiences with the reader. And on these counts, *'A Life Long Romance with Nature and the Wild'* comes high. A unique feature of this work is that the author almost re-tells the stories contained in various chapters through sketches done by him delicately and deftly. This embellishment, I think, the reader should find specially enjoyable. A Life Long Romance' stands out as a collection of hunting (shikar) stories with a difference.

It has been seen that sensitive and right-minded *shikaris*, almost always turn into ardent conservationists in later life. So has Col. Vijay Verma!

SD Singh
(Ex Principal Scindia School Gwalior (MP))

Fig. 6 : The cattle lifter of Kinor- is on his kill- bufflo killed by him.

Fig. 5 : A Peacock calling from a tree before soroting down for the night.

1

Romance with Wild Life and Forest and Real Vintage Stories

The cattle lifter of Kinor

The year was 1946, a year prior to independence my father was the Senior Civil Administrator in *Mandla* district of old CP (Central Province) now Madhya Pradesh.

Kinor village consisting of about 150 huts was mainly inhabited by poor *Gond* tribals. In the recent past, there was a continuous barrage of messages and reports about a very large tiger, who was regularly killing village cattle. The village headman Mallu, an old friend of my father's, from previous visits to his beautiful village sat on the *gound* with folded hands. "*Sahib,* this time this *badmash* (tiger) has killed my precious milk buffalo, she was giving 15 *kilos* of milk a day, and he has become so bold that he came inside the cattle-pen, and chose her, being the fattest and best looking animal, killed and dragged her out of the village into the forest about 500 yards; this was early in the morning at about 3 a.m.; he could not eat much, as the day light is early in the summer. I have covered the *gara* (tiger kill) with ***saal*** leaves and branches, so that the vultures do not finish it off, and I have also made a *machan* on a *saal* tree near the kill. Have you dragged or disturbed the kill in any way, asked my father? No *Sahab,* I know that this tiger is so cunning that he will not return to the kill if it is dragged or disturbed in anyway, luckily the tree in which I have made the *machan* is ideally located for the purpose. If you come by 5 p.m, and sit up, he is bound to come. It was 10 a.m.; the village was about 15 miles from *Mandla* where we lived. Myself, my elder brother Ashok, were also listening to the complaints and requests being made to my father by the headman. It was a weekend, Saturday morning, which fact went in favour of the headman. He made up his mind to help the villages of *Kinor* by trying to get rid of this cattle lifter, who must have already killed at least 50. He sat up on the kill by 5 PM, the tiger turned up early by about 8.30 PM. When he took a shot at him, the tiger. Took a few summersaults and generally kicked up a lot of dust before disappearing behind a small *bund* and a fold in the ground not very far from the *machan;* about 30 yards or so. After some silence, he resumed making angry noises *Roaorouoooangrrr*!! and seemed to be clawing and biting something within his reach, renting his fury and temper on whatever was within reach. In the morning, we found the object of his fury, a young *saal* tree about six-inch thick, clawed and bitten thin to an extent that it was standing upright because it was supported by the other neighbouring trees branches, as soon as it was pushed a bit, it crashed to the ground as if it was cut by an axe. The tiger had obviously been wounded badly by my fathers shot at night; and had moved out of the vicinity after he had exhausted himself, clawing and biting the green *saal* tree, in the early hours of the morning.

Father got down from the tree and *machan* on which he had spent all night, when it was day light and was already examining the area of the kill to make out as to what had happened last night when he was joined by the village headmen and the local *shikari.* The local *shikari, Kappu* was a real expert and extremely sharp in his observations; he soon found some fresh bone pieces with blood and hair, and announced that the tiger was hit most probably in the rear leg, and the main bone above the rear leg joint was badly

Fig. 7 : One of the tigers near leg is but he is charging my father who can be seen-shooting him.

shattered by the soft nose bullet. As seen later on, his observations were absolutely correct. After waiting for about two hours for the summer sun to take its effect on the wounded tiger, my father decided to follow it up and try to end the misery of the tiger.

Following up a wounded tiger is one of the most hazardous tasks imaginable. A tiger once wounded becomes extremely dangerous as he becomes very single minded in destroying his tormentor, and despite the wound it may be handicapped with, can be so full of fury and anger that most humans, who live through the experience can never forget the terror it induces.

Father made sure that all the villagers and other distractions were kept out of the way; he did not even wait for the village cattle to re-assemble in a herd and be driven to the wounded tiger, so that it becomes easier for the hunter to locate the animal in the bushes or where he is lying up. He decided to do this as the area was fairly open and did not have too many bushes and underbrush for cover, except the *saal* trees, flame of the forest and occasional mango and *jamun* tree, it being close to human habitation.

After following the blood trail for about 1 miles, the blood drops seemed to peter off, but were there, where ever the tiger sat down to rest. They soon reached an area where there was a slight crest on one side and small *nullahs* or ravines were running out of this crest line for a few hundred yards, the whole area was covered with rough gravel and sparse yellow grass, barely one to two feet high; as soon as they came up on the east end of this crest, they heard a low growl growlgrrrrrrrrrr!! of the tiger, not very close but not very far either; my father came up on the crest to show himself and try to make the tiger do the same. This was enough to make the tiger furious, who whipped around and charged, from about 40 to 50 yards away, where he was probably resting in one of the ravines, fortunately for my father, the tiger stumbled a bit due to his hind leg, which was shattered so badly and barely, hanging by the skin, bone sticking out (see drawing), he stood his ground and fired 3 deliberately aimed shots into the body of the tiger, with his 405 under liver Winchester rifle; before the tiger fell down barely ten yards away from him.

He was a very strong and well-built tiger, must have weighed atleast 500 to 600 kg, did not have a very long tail but was massively built.

The villagers of *Kinor* were happy to see the end of this dangerous cattle lifter. The car was about 1 1/2 miles from the place, and to carry this heavy weight so far was going to be a tough task.

The headman soon got the men together to get this job done; two stout saplings and some rope were organised and the tiger tied up with some difficulty, then with much huffing and puffing, the carrying party started moving towards the parked car. Some where near the mid-way point, the forward movement was suddenly halted; there was a "Y" fork in the track which was passing through a wooded part of the footpath leading to the parked car, now about 200 yards away, suddenly there was a murmer and a hush, someone muttered in a whisper *"raste mein bagh hai, chup raho!"*. There is a tiger on the path, keep quiet"! Imagine; a huge tiger (a cattle lifter)" had been finally tracked, followed up and then shot when he had made a full blooded charge, and here was another huge male tiger, in broad day light. My father who had done some real rapid and accurate shooting only 1/2 an hour back, was in no mood to shoot another tiger, he simply got his weapon ready, but was not going to shoot another tiger, especially not knowing if he was also a cattle lifter. He just motioned to the men, to keep quiet and stand still; he was barely 25 yards away; the tiger just calmly turned around and walked away after some anxious moment. Perhaps he had come to pay his last respects to a fallen comrade! This

Fig. 8 : The cattle lifter of Kinor being carried to the car when enroute another tiger was seen.

incident is mentioned here to show the readers the number of tigers which were around in 1946 just a year before independence.

2

Espirit-de-corps

"A story of two gallant officers, who stood by each other in adversity"

This is a saga of raw courage, shown under the most adverse conditions, by two Army officers, to stand up against odds for each other.

It brings out the ultimate qualities of leadership, that is to do ones duty under the most stressful and adverse physical and mental conditions imaginable. To do ones bit, no matter what, for ones comrade, to save him and not to save yourself, the ultimate achievement in comradeship and *espirit-de-corps*.

The Indian Military Academy at Dehradun (IMA), during 1955 had two fine young officers on their training staff; a Lt. Col. Gahlot (Infantry) and a Major Gill (a gunner). Both full of *josh* and spirit of adventure. They both also happened to be members of the *Shikar* Club, which then functioned in the IMA.

During one of the training camps in the summer of 1955. The two officers mentioned, were in the camp and had just come into the officers mess after a hot March in the scorching sun, for a well deserved glass of beer; when Major Gill (the officer in charge *Shikar* Club) was informed that, *'Nathu'* the professional *Shikari* employed by the IMA *Shikar* Club at Dehradun region wanted to have a word with him, urgently. Major Gill instead of going out to meet *Nathu,* called him in the mess tent, as there were no other officers around, except Col. Gahlot, who was a keen *shikari* and sportsman. *Nathu* had brought news of a tiger kill, which had taken place in the nearby *Karba pani* block, barely two miles from the mess tent. He had also taken due care not to disturb the area and had managed to put up a *machan* in case one of the officers, would like to sit up for the tiger. He also added, that, the tigress, it was a female, from what he could make out from the pug marks, would come early to feed, as, she was not able to feed on her kill, as it was made just before day light hours and was quite near from the jungle track maintained by the forest department. The young cow killed by the tigress was one of the stragglers from the village herd from nearby *sundarbani,* the villagers used to illegally use as the feeding ground for their cattle by entering the reserve forest in the day and leave by the evening, so that the cattle were safe from tiger and sometime the leopards making a meal of one of them, like on this occasion. Both these officers, though very keen to bag a tiger, had no experience of tiger shooting. Though members of the *shikar* club, their experience was limited to the *murghi* shoots and some time a duck shoot, once or twice a *Chital* Stag was the biggest game shot by either. *Nathu,* spoke up and asked Maj. Gill, if Gentlemen Cadet Ashok Verma (my elder brother) the president of the *shikar* club, could be called, as he was an experienced person in this sport. Both the officers were tempted to call in Ashok to help in this serious matter of going to sit up for a tiger. Ultimately, he was not permitted to come away from his training schedule; so it was that finally, the inexperienced Col. Gahlot and Maj. Gill, both decided to sit up on the kill and bag the tiger. Both lacked the experience but made up for it by their eagerness and enthusiasm. Both armed with double barreled weapons from the IMA, *shikar* club, sat up and were duely briefed by *Nathu,* to be very quiet and make no disturbance till 10 pm; by which time the tigress would surely come.

At about 9 pm there was a fusillade of rifle shots, "Bang-bang-bang- bang". The tigress had turned up on the kill at about nine and started feeding. Major Gill had a torch light, which was not very bright; although they could not see the tiger clearly, they soon could make out the eyes of the tiger in the dim light, so they aimed approximately and fired; in the confusion that followed, they both fired 4 rifle shots, but were not sure if they hit the tiger. They were back in camp by 10 pm. Next morning, *Nathu* who had a nasty suspicion that they had wounded the tigress, requested the officers to get G.C. Verma from the camp nearby and proceed further; but for some reason the officers did not listen to him. They thought that they would accomplish the task themselves. When they visited the vicinity of the kill along with *Nathu,* they soon discovered that the tigress was definitely wounded by one of their shots; as there was plenty of blood and a small piece of bone or two, it was not easy to make out exactly how badly the tigress was wounded.

However, in spite of protests from *Nathu* the two officers insisted in following up the tiger. *Nathu* followed the blood trail for about a mile or two into some thick *Karonda* bushes; from the frequency of the small droplets of the blood flow, it appeared that it was a head wound. The *Karonda* bushes were very thick and was a dangerous place to follow up a wounded tiger as, visibility was very poor due to thick under growth, just when *Nathu* was discussing some alternative plan, the tiger, who was nearby, on hearing human voices, charged them, making furious noises, *"growl-grr, growl"* from about 25 yards, although both Maj. Gill and Col. Gahlot could see the furious and agitated movement of bushes and could here the angry noises made by the tiger, they could not see the body of the tiger clearly, as it was effectively hidden by the thick *Karonda* under brush. Due to their inexperience or call it lack of patience, they fired both barrels off, (their respective rifles), at the charging tiger. Apparently they both missed, and before they could reload, the tiger was out of the bushes and had caught hold of Maj. Gill, who grappled with her, he could make out that there was something wrong with the tiger's mouth; as discovered later; the lower jaw-bone of the tiger had been shattered by the chance rifle shot, due to which her jaw was not working and just hanging by the skin and flesh, perhaps, it was this that saved their life as she could not make a fatal bite. As the tigress was trying to bite the left arm of Maj. Gill and trying to claw at him and cause maximum damage, she saw, this other person (Col. Gehlat) trying frantically to reload his jammed rifle; the peripheral vision of Carnivore like tiger, are very strong; the movements made by Col. Gahlot attracted her attention. She now left Maj. Gill who was down and fighting her, she jumped and then caught hold of Col. Gehlot who was frantically trying to reload his jammed weapon. When Maj Gill was thus, free of the tiger pinning him down inspite of being quite badly wounded and bleeding caused by the clawing and biting efforts of the wounded tigress, he got up, limped up to his empty rifle lying a few feet from him; inspite of a badly chewed left arm (the bone was not crushed as the jaw bone of the tiger was not able to bite through, due to its injury). He reloaded his weapon with a great effort, walked up to the tiger, he dared not fire his weapon from a distance for fear of hitting Col. Gehlot, as the tigress was on top him, covering most of his body , clawing and biting at his colleague, put the muzzle of the weapon on the main body of the tiger and fired, killing her.

Nathu was watching this grim drama being played from the safety of a *saal* tree, which he had hastily climbed as soon as he heard the blood curdling noises of the tigress, when she made her charge. He soon got down from the tree, when Maj. Gill shouted at him to come down and get help quickly, the tiger was dead, fortunately the camp ambulance and doctor on duty was at hand and was able to attend to

Fig. 9 : The tigeress was wounded in the jaw therefore could not bite Maj Gehlot, who is pinned down by her Maj Grill is Seen loading his weapon before finally shooting the wounded tigress.

their wounds inflicted by the tigress on both the officers by her claws, fortunately due to the jaw bone being broken by the chance shot over the kill she could not bite. Claw wounds of a tiger can be very dangerous, as they cause dangerous infection due to rotting flesh bacteria ever present in them.

This tigress was skinned and duely hung up in the Gentlemen cadets' cafe at the IMA, Dehradun after it was mounted and cured by Van ingnes and Van ingnes, Mysore - the only taxidermists in India at that time.

But I somehow always felt that the brave actions of these two officers who inspite of the grave injuries to themselves and inspite of the danger involved, not only followed up the wounded tiger, but also finished the job of killing her, ending her misery, by the wound caused by the chance shot over the kill. Their actions, while they were under attack from the wounded tiger were nothing short of exemplary, that inspite of being injured badly by the tiger, they helped each other and finished the job successfully. They both exhibited great courage and a very high level of *espirit-de-corps*. An ideal to be emulated by the young gentleman cadets, soon to become officers themselves.

Note : *Although this story is based on wildlife experiences of the subjects, but the qualities displayed under dire circumstances by the officers concerned, were very similar which might exist on a battlefield. Both the officers mentioned in this episode, went on to become Generals later.*

*see *last chapter, on conservation, the decline in there numbers was fairly rapid after the time of this story was written.*

Fig. 14 : Difference between African buffloe and a Indian buffaloe

3

Vengeance will be mine!

"A story of 'kana' The rogue wild buffalo"

Both the species of wild buffalo, Indian and the one found in Africa are different in many physical aspects; most obvious being the shape and sweep of its horns. In the Indian buffalo it is like a scimitar or curved broad sword, coming towards its back and is much more in length as its African cousin, which are embossed, almost half round, thick base in the centre of the forehead curving or curling down side ways and the tips being curved upwards, (*See - sketch*). However, all sportsmen who have hunted these two deadly customers, agree that both these species have one thing in common and that is its outstanding courage, viciousness, cunning and the ability to put the fear of god in anyone, who dares to hunt it and then only succeeds in wounding it. When being followed up, after it is wounded, all the deadly characteristics mentioned above, appear to increase many fold in this animal. The following narrative of a true story brings out the grim prospects of following up a wounded buffalo.

The story goes back to 1934, Bilaspur district of then (CP) Central Provinces, later (MP) Madhya Pradesh and now Jharkhand. At that time, the Indian buffalo was found in fair numbers in that region of our country. (See map)

A famous big game hunter and a British Police Oficer, SP of Bilaspur, a Mr Stewart (a bachelor) had been posted in Bilaspur for the last eight years or so and was a well known gentleman and was known as a no nonsense police officer as well as a very friendly and genial person, particularly with the *Baigha* tribesmen in North Bilaspur. He spent many of his annual leaves there hunting big game (since he was a bachelor, he did not go home on long leave like his married friends but preferred to spend his time in hunting, mainly big game in the beautiful *saal* and bamboo forest, of Bilaspur and Raipur. This incident occurred during one such hunt. Mr Stewart had camped for some days with his personal staff and was in touch with the local *Baigha* tracker and *shikari Biggu,* who had just brought news of the big single bull buffalo, *Kana,* (or squint eyed as he was known, due to being blind in one eye, which he had lost in a fight with another bull buffalo, two years back). He had been after this particular animal which was known for his aggressive nature, cunning and size of his big horns, his head was a prized trophy. He had recently killed a village male buffalo, who came near to a female domestic buffalo, in whom '*Kana*' the wild one was currently interested romantically! This was quite a common occurrence in the villages which were in the domain of the wild buffaloes.

Stewart made a quick appreciation of the situation and in consultation with *Biggu* the tracker and decided to go after the buffalo.

On reaching the village where the domestic buffalo was killed by *Kana,* he learnt from the villagers that most probably the wild one was still in the vicinity, but would soon leave, as there were no more domestic buffalo in season in the small herd in this village. He decided to rest at the village for the night and start in the morning to locate him.

It was a cold dry morning of January 1934, except for the heavy dew which lasted till 10 or 11 am in the winter months which made the earth moist, due to which tracking

Fig. 11 : The buffloe (Kana) sitting among the bull rushes

of a heavy animal was easier from the more prominent tracks. *Biggu* was hopeful of catching up with the buffalo by mid-day, if the wind remained favourable, we may even sight the animal, he told Stewart.

It was almost 2:00 pm, almost eight hours of continuous, monotonous, tracking. *Biggu* knew Stewart, from many hunting trips, that he would never digress from his main aim which was now to get the big buffalo. Though they came across many other good heads of *chital, sambhar and wild boar,* but he would never shoot any of these animals for fear of alarming his main query, *Kana,* the buffalo, who seemed close now.

The big bull was heading for a mud pond and marsh which was now very close; *Biggu* warned Stewart about the likelihood of the big bull cooling off in the mud pond after a long trek in the sun. As they approached the pond, *Biggu* pointed out the big hoofs of the bull, near the pond, leading straight into the pond, which was about 100 sq. yards, overgrown with bull-rushes and tall grass. At first they could just see some white cattle egrets hunting for tad-poles on the edge of the pond; a grey heron, intent on some mud fish; a jungle crow flew overhead, "CAWW- CAWW .... " his harsh call sounded bizzare and lonesome; suddenly there was a sinister silence, both *Biggu* and Stewart sensed that something dangerous was watching them; the jungle crow flew in a circle and came low over a thicket in the bull rushes where the pond seemed deepest; they both saw the slight turn of the head, and the scimitar shaped huge horns of the buffalo emerge from among the thin bull rushes. The bull was sitting in the mud, his body submerged; the crow had warned, the buffalo as well as the trackers of each other.

His reputation was of always being aggressive towards humans but even the toughest of rogues in the forests, like the lone bull elephants and buffaloes like this one, have a sixth sense of survival and self- preservation, which warns them that this pair tracking him and who have disturbed him in his mud bath are no ordinary villagers, but a danger to him. Instead of charging them as expected, he started to hurry out of the mud and head towards the thick *saal* and *bamboo* forest on the opposite side of the pond. As he was lumbering out of the quagmire and thick cover of the bull rushes, Stewart saw him clearly, nose up, horns swept back heading towards the forests; he had seen this site before on two occasions, when this bull ran off like this, he never saw him again, in spite of best efforts. It was this last fear of the bull disappearing that probably made him take a quick shot at the bull, against his better judgment. It was a shot from behind, on a moving target, away from him. Although the bull never broke his stride on being fired upon, but the way he paused for a moment, before he entered the forest, now about 200 yards, it appeared that he had been hit. *Biggu* was soon on the trail of the bull, Stewart told him that, he is hard hit and will not get away very far. *Biggu,* soon picked up a blade of grass with thick fresh blood mixed with mud and slime, look *sahib,* it has bubbles in it; he is definitely hard hit and close to the lungs.

The time was about 2:30 pm but being winter, the light would be good for shooting for another three hours or so, say up to 5:30 pm; but they had not reckoned with the further gloom caused by the dark bamboo and *saal* forest, into which the bull was heading.

In the heat of the chase, many things are overlooked, which ultimately lead to disaster, as things turned out.

This was the point up to which, more than one witness had seen, Stewart *sahib* and *Biggu;* the *Baiga* villagers who had followed the two from the village, where the bull had been visiting the domestic buffalo and had killed one of there male buffalo. On hearing the shots, they (villagers) rushed up to the pond and stopped short of the pond from where they could see the *sahib* and *Biggu,* examine the ground and then enter the forest after some discussion. They new that the bull was wounded and now the hunters were trying

Fig. 12 : The buffaloe sitting out of the pond and heading for the forest when it was shot and wounded.

to follow it up for finishing him off. They also new that it was no ordinary task to follow up a wounded buffalo bull and that too a nasty bull like this one known as a *Kana* (the squint eyed one).

My father (a bachelor at that time) had just joined the civil service as one of the youngest SDO'S in *Bilaspur* district. In just under six months, his Collector and other British Officers who were his colleagues but also his bosses, had developed a great respect for him due to his straight forward nature and down to earth ways.

He was woken up at mid-night and urgently summoned by the Collector. He soon reached the Collectors bunglow, not very far from his quarters. There he recognised the local *shikari* and tracker *Biggu* squatting on the ground - with a constable (Policeman in uniform) standing next to him. The DC did not waste much time on formalities and came to the point straight away. He addressed my father directly and handed him a solar pith *topi* (hat), worn by most British Officer those days to protect themselves from the sun. This man *Biggu* (the tracker) turned up at the police station about 30 minutes back with this hat and claims that this hat belonged to Mr Stewart, the SP; whom, he claims that a wild buffalo had killed last night. Now, I know that Stewart, started his annual leave, three days back and I also know that he was preparing to go on a big game hunt soon, and now, this....!

Now this happens to be in your Sub-division, Mr Verma, so better look sharp and look into this straight away, a senior British Police Officer is, let us say, missing or reported missing. I want an answer to this with-in the shortest possible time. It was thus that it came about that my father was asked to carry out an enquiry into the circumstances, in which Mr Stewart had disappeared. My father had been chosen to do this important inquiry as not only was he already known as a good and just officer by the locals; he had also quickly established himself as a sportsman *shikari,* big game hunter.

My father was soon camping in the *Katla* village, next day by about 3:00 pm. He had accomplished this by forced march with ponies and mules, carrying his camp kit. He soon established from the villagers, up to the point when they heard the rifle shots at the pond and had seen Stewart *sahib* and *Biggu* enter the forest. This was now two days and two nights away after this, the tricky bit of this enquiry started, as the only witness to what followed was *Biggu,* the *Baiga* tracker and *shikari.*

My father decided to, question as many villagers about the evidence so far, carefully note it down; rest for the night and start the important part of the enquiry next morning with *Biggu and Stewart* tracking the wounded animal which was evidence of what happened on the ground. One more thing that was bothering my father was, as to, what had happened to the bull buffalo and where was he now; the answer to this seemed to be that he had died of the wounds inflicted by Mr Stewart on him soon after he had done with him. (he had killed him) *Biggu* was 99 per cent sure that the buffalo had died soon after and about 200 yards away from the spot, where he had killed Mr Stewart.

The story put together by the enquiry:

The two, Mr Stewart and *Biggu* entered the forest on the trail of the wounded Bull Buffalo; look here *sahib,* he sat down here and rested, there is spurt of blood, then, he has stood up and walked, on, this way; the blood is less, it has clogged, may be the mud cake on his back has absorbed the blood.

It was about 5:00 pm now; we had been following *Kana* for almost three hours and must have walked about four to five miles, the forest though dense was not very thick near the floor of the forest. We soon reached the spot where the main gruesome drama had taken place.

Biggu had his eyes glued to the ground, evidence of a blood drop here, a smear on the bush leaves there, this trail

Fig. 10 : The buffalo hiding behind the spaces of creeps before attaching the hunter

apparently carried on in a Northernly direction, parallel to a screen like creeper on and along the East of this trail, *Biggu* was about five paces in front of Mr Stewart, when he looked behind and to the left of Mr Stewart, aghast by what he saw, his mouth opened but he could not shout and no sound came out. He had heard a "SWISH' sound, but it was not the sound of wind blowing through the tall trees. It was a. "SWISH" of a scythe like horns of the bull buffalo. He had been waiting behind the screen like creeper, patiently; he let the tracker and the hunter go past him on his trail; he had circled round his track, coming back in a parallel and circular trail back to his trail and, came to this spot behind this natural screen and then stood patiently and perfectly still for at least 30 minutes; because, he new that the pursuers and his tormentors would pass this way soorer than later. Just after they had gone past his position, he attacked them from behind this screen, with the swiftness of a silent ghost, a master wielder of a scythe, before Mr Stewart could quickly align and shoot, he probably shot him, but, this was not enough to stop the buffalo; with one swipe of his horn's he had flung Mr Stewart into the air, he fell heavily to the ground badly injured and wounded; there, (I was watching this from that tree where I had climbed to save myself). Before Mr Stewart could even move, the bull was on him, goring him and stamping him into the ground; he kept circling him for a good 15-20 minutes attacking him again and again stamping him with his front hoofs and goring him into the earth with his massive horns and head. I made some noise to try to drive him away; he stopped, goring Mr Stewart into the ground, then glared at me, and advanced towards my tree, shaking his head and horns, with up and down motions, snorting through nostrils, indicating what he would do to me if he could get to me. Shivering with freight, I climbed a few feet more on the tree.

When I saw the traces of this terrible drama being played in this jungle theatre by a wounded wild beast and his pursuer, I could imagine, as to what had transpired, ... this is what I wrote in my enquiry.

"The bull buffalo had gone about his gory task of killing Mr Stewart to a point, that one could not tell from the remains of the human body, whether it was a "white", man or a local Indian villager who had been, thus brutally killed. His identity was ascertained by me by examining his shirt pocket and some documents in his wallet, in his back pocket. I have also brought some remains of Mr Stewart, for his relatives, as and when they turn up from England and for examining in the lab for scientific evidence to prove his identity".

The rogue buffalo bull, *"Kana"* after smashing his tormentor into the ground had limped off the scene and soon sat down about 300 yards from the spot, from where he never got up. He died of the wounds from the first shot that Mr Stewart had wounded him with at the pond. It almost appeared that the stout-hearted buffalo held on to life, just to take his revenge; but the exertion of attacking and killing Mr Stewart took its toll on his wounds and he soon succumbed to them and died, but only after he had avenged himself.

Fig. 13 : The buffloe going and killing the hunter, the tracker can be seen having climbed a true to save himself.

4

NAWAB

(The year 1942-43 Jabalpur)

Nawab was the family favourite, he was one among many. There was *bunta* the marbled cat (grey, huge cat with white spots). Several birds i.e. a beautiful peacock with a long flowing tail, like a beautiful train of emerald and deep blue feathers, he had his harem of 3-4 drab looking female peahens; drab looking only when compared to the proud lord and master, who always liked to roost on the top of the house, specially in the morning and evening, when he flew up there with a great flapping of wings, to call *miyaoo / meeyaooo meeyaooo* !! *kuk kuk meeyaooo* !!, a mournful musical call to end and begin a day. Then there were, a few pigeons, mainly the grey mixed with white variety, they definitely had homing instincts, as I remember - some time they were missing from the house all day flying about here and there in the sky, but always being back home in the evenings. The usual red fowls, one red rooster and 5-6 hens, then there were some guinea fowls too (the only non Indian birds they were from Africa). But finally there was this big huge loveable ***anarkali*** the female elephant, she belonged to the forest department but was kept at my father's house. For his tours to the local villages in his sub-division. And finally there was ***nawab,*** the half breed spaniel dog, he was something special, loved by

A pecock and elephant on the night and other animals pet in the Jabalpur house

everyone including the cat *bunta,* but was specially adored by us kids (Meera, Kamla, the elder sisters, Ashok the elder brother, and myself Vijay).

This Story that follows is about *nawab,* it was not only surprising but amazing how these animals particularly, dogs have a homing instinct in the how it works, is amazing?

My father who was SDO at Jabalpur (old CP now MP) had gone on a tour to Damoh, a tehsil of Jabalpur, about 30 miles from Jabalpur. Being a weekend he took us all along with him. All meant mother, four of us kids and of course ***nawab,*** who was always the first to jump into the car when he got the slightest hint of the family going out into the country side. Through out the journey to Damoh, about 30 miles, ***nawab*** was sleeping either on the rear seat with one of us kids or he was pushed down on the floor in the space behind the front seat, he made a nice and soft footmat!

On reaching the vicinity of Damoh, we were guided by villagers and the camp staff to the place where camp had been set up in a mango grove. It being early June, most trees were heavy with fruit (mangoes) of the juicy *(Chusane walla aam)* type. These mangoes looked so good even though raw and sour in taste, but a great attraction for us kids. But father had given strict order's!!! not to pluck any mangoes from the trees as they belonged to the contractor who had bought the fruit on the trees from the owner of the orchard; the same contractor was incharge of setting up camp for the SDOs visit. The mango grove being the only shady place in the vicinity, therefore he had set up the tents, in the cool shade of the large mango trees. One tent (EPIP Type) was already set up, another one or two were being pitched.

It had taken almost two hours to cover 30 miles those day's, the road was metal but had pot holes (the second world war was on -1942-43 - The British Raj was devoting all its energy and money to the war effort in Europe and Burma, the bad roads was only one small side effect! one could see on

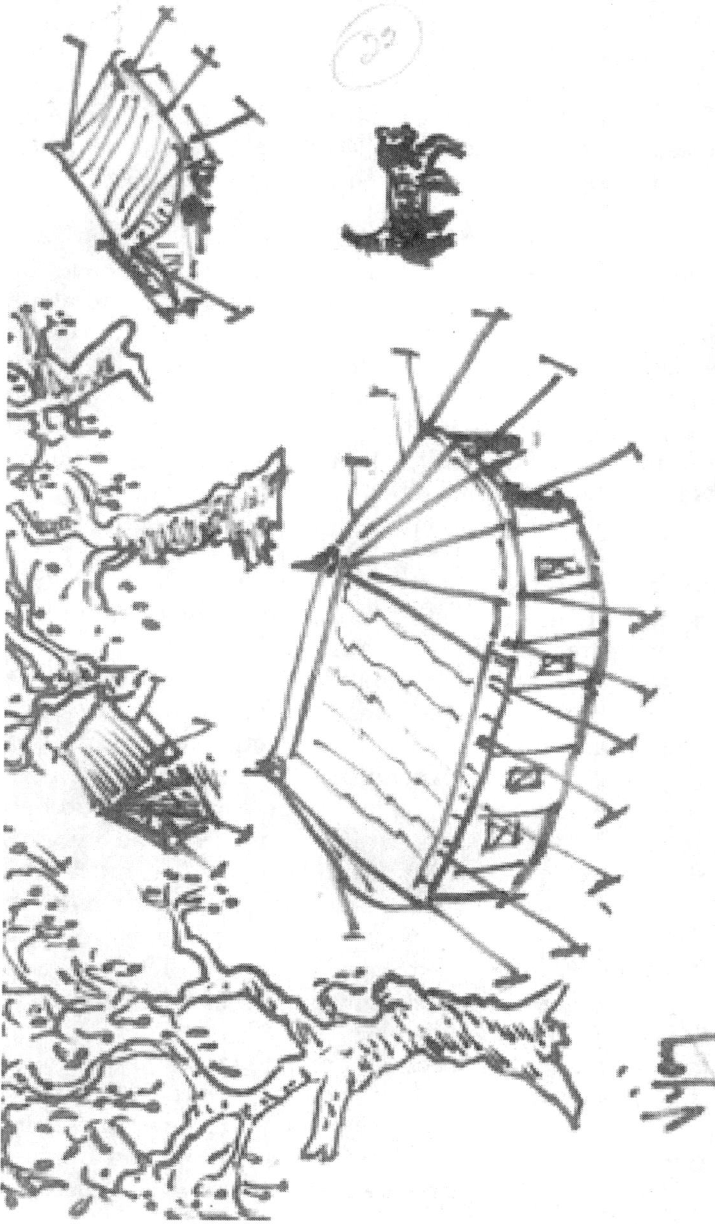

Nawab in the Damoh Camp.

the ground in India). The journey had been bumpy; ***nawab*** was tired, after his usual scouting about in the new place and leg up! Marking of his territory routine, he came and sat down in a living tent where he was told to sit and stay, like a good dog he slept under a table.

Father got busy with his work in the fields, which were a few miles from camp, he had gone in his car. I got bitten by a scorpion *(bicchchu)* while playing, running in and out of the large tents, it was a small one (fortunately for me) hiding in the hay used for cushioning under the *Durri* (carpet). They found it and killed it, after showing it to my mother. She took me to a nearby sorcerer, there was no doctor nearby (within 10 miles), There was no car! No cellphone! I could hardly walk; the pain was intense, shooting up the leg in spasms, right into the thigh and upper regions of the leg. All three, brother and 2 sisters were looking at me in a strange way, why is he making such a big song and dance of pain in his leg, stream of tears and low moans of agony. The truth was that I happened to be the only one, who ever got bitten by a scorpion! So I knew what it meant, they had no idea, because they had not been bitten (lucky for them). With all these tamasha's and fuss going on, over poor me, even the cook his helper, the other help in camp, all were over seeing the village sorcerers antics! Now he had taken charge of me and had put some raw mango oil and juice (it is acidic) on the bitten area, he even made a few pin pricks so that the acidic oil goes through to the scorpion venom which is alkaline and neutralize the venom; it gave me sudden relief, and everybody else also nodded in sympathy and relief. Except ***nawab***, he just kept sleeping under the table, perhaps he curled up even more as a mini storm (common in the summer in India) seemed to be brewing up, which must have muffled any sound people made in the camp area. But poor ***nawab*** when he woke up, when it suddenly went quiet, after the mini storm had passed with thunder and a sharp shower. He walked out of the tent, wagging his tail went into the big tent, he found no one there, no one in the kitchen, no one

Nawab on his way to Jabalpur from Damoh

anywhere; poor fellow must have been frantic, and it is also past my *(**nawab's**)* supper time. It was near 9 P.M., we that is "me the walking wounded" and the whole crowd of sympathizers, now joined by my father, returned to camp by about 9:30 P.M. Patromaxs, lanterns were lit, people were beating the *durries* inside the tents with sticks to shoo away, any more lurking scorpions. By now my pain was much less. I could put my foot down and walk with a limp, of course. I was made comfortable on a camp cot. Soon *Kamla* (the younger of my elder sister's) brought a bowl of soup for me. She is the one who looks after me when I am in pain even now! She has a long standing experience as you can see!

When I was snug and comfortable, some soup in the tummy and the glow of so much attention and sympathy; but someone had not yet sympathized with me! Please *call (**nawab**,* I requested in a weak voice; my first few words, other than the oohs and aahs, noises of pain I had been making. Everybody wanted to call ***nawab*** to come and fuss over me. 1 kept hearing calls, ***nawab*** - ***nawab*** (to call him) than distant shouts - ! ***Nawab*** had vanished disappeared. Everyone forgot about me even I forgot my pain and limped around the tents calling out to ***nawab***. No response. My father was furious with the camp in charge, his peon, then he scolded the contractor who had set up the camp and was standing near by. You better find this dog soon if you know what is good for you. *Shaib,* there is *gulbagh* (a panther) who strays into this area some times, he is known to pick up village dogs. The local *shikari Budhiya Gond* was a friend of my father, who used to accompany him on partridge and green pigeon shoots, after his working day was over. He had showed him leopard pug marks in the bush some times and always was keen for him to shoot one some time. Does he kill your cattle or goats often or only when they stray into the forest, he said, yes, they never or rarely do that, unless our cattle stray into the reserve forest. *Budiya* had heard the contractor trying to put the blame on the local panther, for ***nawab's*** disappearance; he spoke up and said, "No, I have checked all foot paths entering into this mango grove, there are no fresh pug marks of a panther, coming in and going out; I doubt very much if he is the culprit. Father heard him and realized that *Budiya* was right 99% of the times, when it was a problem of this type. Ok then, where could the dog be? Or where could he go and why? we soon found out the answer to this; when after finishing his work on Sunday morning by about 11:00 A.M., and having early brunch, we started our drive back to Jabalpur. It was a hot day, father was driving at a sedate pace to avoid over heating of the car, he even stopped in the shade, which was there all along the road, for a cool drink. After driving for about 2 hours, everyone was feeling very low and sleepy, when father said something loudly enough to wake everybody up; there he is, I think it is ***nawab!!*** He practically stopped there it self, but then covered the rest of 200 yards or so slowly in order not to kick up dust; he stopped near ***nawab***, who was limping, due to blisters, but was steadily walking towards Jabalpur. Now just 10 miles away it was as joyous a reunion as could be, I am not sure who was happier, the dog or us humans to have been reunited after this mysterious disappearance of the dog from camp.

But the question of this uncanny and great ability of the dog to be heading home from a distant, unknown place was nothing short of a miracle, perhaps something akin to migratory birds or homing pigeons.*

*This instinct which definitely was there in dogs seems to be missing in dogs now, especially in small breeds, who easily get lost in towns in built up areas and cannot find there way back.

Fig. 15 : Cobra can he seen in the pee-pot

5

The Cobra in the Pee Pot!

(Katni, 1944)

The jungle *dakbungalow* of Khatauli was still a few miles away; and it was nearing lunch time. A hot lunch of fresh eggs (real organic red fowl egg!) made into an omelet and hot *parontha's,* with green chilly and raw onion, and if lucky a glass of milk or *chai.* I was not only eagerly looking forward to lunch but was also wanting to - you know - !! go to the rest room urgently. When we were still a little distance away from the *dakbunglow* (rest house), the *chowkidaar* (the caretaker of the place - also doubled as the *khansama* or cook) was opening up the doors of the rest house on hearing the horn of the car, he was expecting us also. As soon as the car entered the gate and came to standstill in front of the *verandah,* I opened the doors and dashed in for the bathroom; the bathroom doors was open and there was this Pee Pot on a small wooden stool in the corner with a lid, all made of enameled metals (the pots for the big job as well as small). You see there were no flush system, so there were these thunder boxes, as we called them, and these Pee pots!. All the cleaning up was done manually later on. Meanwhile everything had a lid or a cover . Yes, so I was in a big hurry and rushed into the bathroom; and whoosh! A cobra (snake) stands up, from the pot in all its majesty and ferocious intent to strike anybody, who has dared to disturb him! Fortunately for me, my reflexes were pretty good - I took a double jump (like in hop step and jump) backwards and gave a loud yelp. It was a loud *Saaanp!! Saaanp!!!* (snake - snake) shout. My father who always had his shot-gun handy in the jungle area, in old CP now MP; came in a hurry; asking me to be calm and be quiet and tell him where the snake was; I told him, it is in the pee pot in the bathroom. As soon as father tapped the door of the open bathroom door, the cobra again lifted its hood clearly six inches above the rim of the pot. Father was about to shoot the cobra, when he heard the quiet request from behind; the *chowkidaar* (watchman) making a humble request; *Sahib* (Sir) don't kill him, he is harmless, in fact he looks after this *dakbungalow* by keeping, the monkeys away and yes, the big rats, which cause havoc otherwise. He is big, black and looks menacing at times, but he has never bitten anyone. My father hearing this, lowered his gun; sure enough the big snake, soon slithered out of his resting place in the pot, and came out of the bathroom, ignored all the humans in the living and dining room, majestically went across the floor of the room straight for the open door, on to the *verandah*, slithered down the *verandah* steps, about three feet high and made for the bamboo clump on one side of the *dakbungalow* compound fence, about 25 yards away, and disappeared from view.

My wife often leaves a saucer of milk for him, near that big *peepal* tree (holy tree in India), which he always drinks, he is our *Naag Devta* (snake God) and our protector.

The Cobra can be seen slithring away towards the bamboo bushes, without harming anyone.

6

The Man Eating Leopard of *Jhilpa*

(Near Nagpur 1942-43)

The Leopards of Nagpur: Of all the experiences in the forests with wild game, encounters with leopards have been some of the most thrilling and memorable. My earliest memories of these spotted beauties were with the leopards around Nagpur in the old Central Provinces, now a part of Maharashtra, India.

My father was in the Indian Administrative Service and was posted at Nagpur in 1942-45; he was SDO in-charge of *Savner* and *Katol tehsils*, part of Nagpur district. He toured the villages during the course of his duties, and my brother and I frequently accompanied him on these tours. Leopards were numerous in those areas at that time and it was part of my father's duties to listen to the villagers problems caused by the frequent attacks of these leopard and rid them of this menace when possible.

The countryside around Nagpur was dotted with orange orchards in between the villages there were deep *nullahs* (streams). The water flow was seasonal but it always left a few pools of water at places, even when the *nullahs* dried up during summer. It was in the thicket along these *nullahs*, mainly consisting of *'Sindri'*, date palms at various stages of growth, ber, lantana bushes and at times even small patches of typical Madhya Pradesh open forest – sparse and dry deciduous forests consisting of teak and flame of the forest trees and other bushes – that provided suitable cover for the leopard. Due to lack of natural game like deer and wild boar

The leopard had hung up not one but two kills on the tree.

which had been depleted in numbers by the villagers poaching for meat, they often preyed on the village live stock, mainly dogs, goats and even cattle.

My first memory of seeing a leopard kill was of a small cow, hung up on a tree. As a youngster, I was very adept at climbing trees, so I climbed up the tree to take a closer look at the calf. I wanted to see for myself how the job of hanging an animal, which must have weighed at least 80 to 100 kgs, was accomplished so neatly and securely. The motive of the leopard taking this ingenious step of hanging up his dinner was to prevent scavengers like jackals and vultures feeding on it. To carry up such a heavy load into the higher reaches of a tree and then hang up the kill on a fork of a stout branch, was nothing short of a juggler's performance and an exhibition of raw strength. On another occasion, the leopard had hung up not just one kill, but two kills. It was like having a larder of meat hanging in his backyard.

The village headman had already erected a *machan* on a suitable tree near the latest kill for my father to take up vigil. The only snag of sitting up on that *machan* was that it was on the same level–as the kills, which were hung up on the tree. And this is exactly what went wrong as events unfolded.

The leopard returned to the kill at about 7 p.m. when there was still plenty of light, being summer, there was still at least half an hour more of day light left. He came from behind some bushes on the high ground from right of the *machan*. As he approached he kept looking up, obviously to check on the kills hung up in the tree. He immediately spotted the *machan* and the human figure camouflaged in it. Before my father could align his sights for a shot, the leopard was off with a bound. Since the leopard had seen him, there was no point in continuing to sit up, he returned to spend the night in the nearby village.

The leopard had been obviously watching from behind cover as we later discovered on inspection of the kills the next morning. Sometimes during the night it had brought down one of the kill and had a good feed.

The leopards in these parts were quite numerous. This was evident from the fact whichever village we visited, there were always one or two reported to be in the region. I would estimate the number of leopards in the tehsils of *Savner* and *Katol* to be about 20 to 30, at that time – 1942-45.

There were two types of leopards, although basically the same species, but the difference was in the size and habits of these leopards and the type of animals they preyed on, and the way the kill was eaten.

The smaller variety, generally referred to as panther, was of a smaller size (about six to seven feet in length). These generally preyed on the village dogs, goats and sometimes calves of cows and buffaloes. These animals were dirty eaters, in that, they always ate the stomach entrails of the killed animal first when starting to feed on a fresh kill.

The larger ones commonly called leopards were more than seven to eight feet in length and generally preferred to stick to the more remote areas of the forests in the region. These leopards were clean eaters, always starting to eat from the fleshy part of the rear legs or buttocks of a fresh kill – similar to a tiger. Curiously, in these parts the leopards were more numerous. Even in those days, my father was basically a conservationist, as he never undertook to shoot a leopard, unless the destruction of the villager's livestock was more than normal, and the leopard was a confirmed cattle lifter. The leopard which hung up its kills on a tree was one of them, which he finally shot by outwitting him, by sitting up for him on the ground behind some bushes, near the tree where the kill was hung up.

The story that follows is about a leopard that became a man-eater and terrorised the poor villagers of this region for a long time.

Jhilpa was a small village in the midst of the leopard country described in the above paragraph, in *Katol* Tehsil about 30 miles, from Nagpur. The story of a man-eating leopard named after this village is unusual. It is interesting to note that when a leopard starts to kill human beings, it makes kills only under cover of darkness and uses all its cunning and guile to get its prey, whereas, a tiger turned man-eater hunts its prey even in daylight. The animal's natural fear of humans has gone, but it's sixth sense tells it that it has to be doubly on guard, in order not to be caught unaware by this dreaded yet easy two legged prey. It knows from experience about all the tricks these human's are up to, like sitting up on kills or poisoning them and so forth.

As a result, a man-eating leopard rarely returns to a human kill. Both the tiger and the leopard are basically nocturnal hunters and prefer the cover of nightfall to hunt, as their nightvision is far more superior to their prey; especially so in case of human prey, once they turn man-eaters. But this boldness in case of the mighty tiger to attack humans in daylight hours brings out the difference in the character of the two animals; the tiger, bold and fearless, king of the jungles and the leopard, cunning, treacherous, devilish and like a ghost in the night.

The Jhilpa man-eater was truly a beautiful, huge and a perfect specimen of a forest leopard. It was a mystery as to how and why it became a man-eater. It is a well- known fact that carnivore- both tigers and leopards take to man as their prey only when they are driven to it, due to some injury, generally caused by (humans) hunting or porcupine quills which makes it difficult for it to hunt its natural prey. But this magnificent animal was without a single blemish on its limbs or its limbs or on its fine coat of yellow and black rosettes. No wonder, after this huge and healthy animal was shot, doubts were initially expressed about its identity as to whether it was the actual man-eater. However, the fact was soon confirmed, since no further human kills were reported from the area after its death.

The only possible explanation for the leopard becoming a man-eater was that there had been a cholera epidemic in this region a few years ago when people had died in large numbers. Firewood to cremate the dead was scarce and expensive; so the poor villagers merely completed the religious rites by putting a burning coal or two in the mouth of the dead and then dispose off the body by throwing it in the ravines or in the beds of *nullah*s bordering most villages.

As it is always hard work for leopard and tigers to stalk and kill there natural food, they never leave any carrion or dead meat which they come across. It is quite possible that this leopard came across these dead bodies and being hungry must have fed on them. It had a regular supply of this new-found food, till the epidemic lasted, which was for about three months. After which the supply of human dead bodies must have petered out. Having got accustomed to human flesh, it must have been then that it started to kill humans and found them to be an easy prey.

The man-eater terrorised a vast area, approximately two to three thousand square miles, consisting of several small and large villages scattered in the area, interspersed with scraggy wild country; orange orchards and scrub forests. The means of communication was mainly by bullock cart; some of the villages were only connected by foot tracks. Though remote, the government postman did manage to visit them once a month.

In all, the 160 or so reported human kills, during its reign of terror in the tehsils of Katol and Savner in the Nagpur district, the Jhilpa leopard was never known to have returned to a human kill for a second feed, as leopards do as a matter of habit when they kill their normal prey. As a result, it always made a heavy first meal of its human kills, whenever it got the chance to do so. It also uncannily disappeared from the area for long periods after it had made a human kill, after having fed on it or sometimes even after it had to abandon the kill due to it being forced to leave it intact; as in some instances the villagers were able to muster up enough courage to follow up the blood trail at night with the help of crude torches made from burning sticks and straw; the only weapons they had to defend themselves were wooden bamboo stakes or sometimes spears and machetes (light and sharp axes commonly carried by villagers to chop wood). Under the circumstances, we always admired the courage of the villagers following the man-eater with their crude weapons to ward off an attack by the leopard, it is well known how fiercely the big cats defend their kills against any intrusion.

The leopard operated mainly in the smaller villages. The poor villager's huts were generally made from wood and grass, matted with a mixture of cow dung and mud, all in all a flimsy structure. On several occasions it just pawed a hole in the roof and got in and out the same way, with its kill. Most doors of the huts bore its claw marks. On one occasion it climbed up a *machan*, where a man was stationed to protect the crops from wild boar and neelgai at night. Luckily, the man was asleep with his head covered with a blanket and this saved his life. The leopard grabbed the blanket and dragged it away, giving the man a chance to escape.

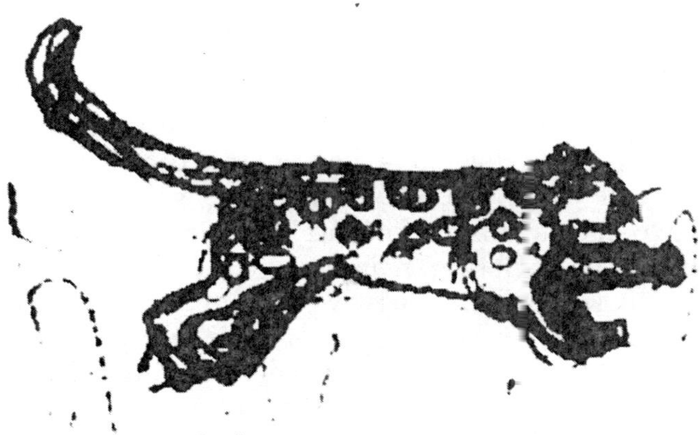

A panther on the run.

On another occasion, it was blood curdling to observe how absolutely silently the leopard chose its prey. In the hut, which it had entered through a small opening between the roof and the wall of the hut, there was a family of four sleeping on the floor, a young woman, Anjibai, Rane her husband and their two children Joli (six years) and Antu (two years). The woman, whom the leopard chose and killed, was in the middle of the sleeping groups. The killing was done so expertly and silently that it was only in the morning, when the husband woke up that he discovered the terrible truth from the few drops of dried blood left on the floor of the hut and the slightly enlarged gap between the wall and the roof, through which the leopard had taken Anijbai away.

My father sat up all night over the half-eaten body of the woman after having persuaded the bereaved husband to allow him to do so, and take the slim chance of avenging his wife's killer. As always, it never showed up. But made another kill in a village called Jhilpa, a few miles away. My father had been camping in the region for about six weeks and had constantly been on the trail of this leopard, but the latter always seemed to be a jump ahead of him and had been very elusive.

However, the leopard's presence in the area had one good effect. The villagers had become more alert and were in a fighting mood; the mere presence of the SDO ***sahab*** and his party in their village was a big morale booster. They were now ready to help in whatever way they could to get rid of this dreaded terror and menace on their doorsteps; living in constant fear of losing their dear ones, as long as the spotted devil lived, their fear always mounted with the onset of darkness. As a result, the man-eater was finding it more and more difficult to make human kills. The latest victim of the leopard was a young boy, who went out early in the morning to relieve himself. The boy saw the leopard before it pounced on him and shouted for help. On hearing the boy's screams, some of the men who had been deputed for this type of situation, immediately came out with lanterns, torches, lathis, spears and drums. They were soon on the leopard's trail. It was able to drag and carry the boy 100 yards or so, when the shouting mob seemed to be on it, it left the boy and bolted. Thus, it could not feed on its latest kill, and remained hungry.

The last human kill it had fed on was now 12 days earlier. Although it had killed again it could not feed on it. This was an encouraging factor in this grim cat and mouse game with the man-eater.

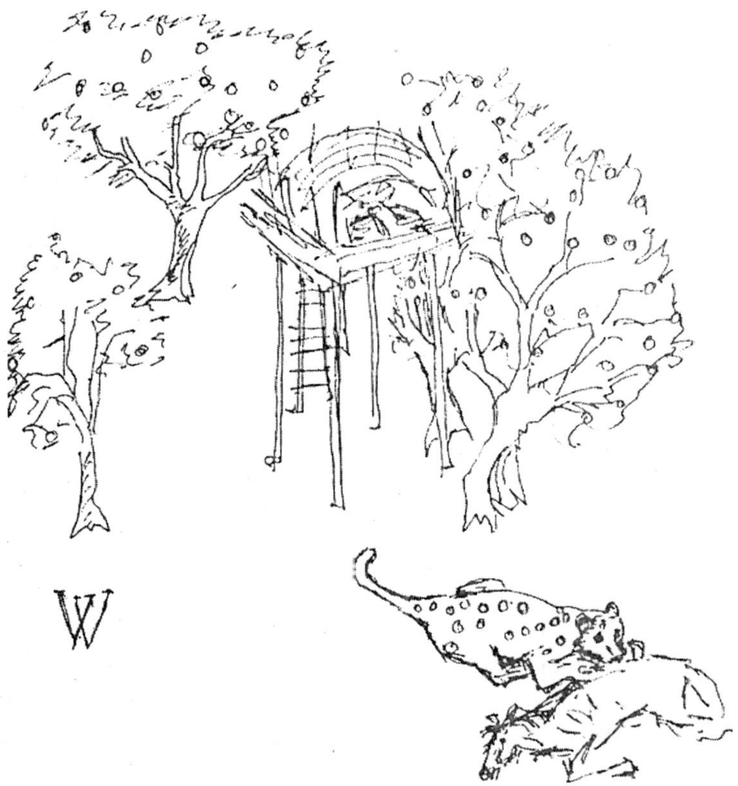

The *machan* in the orange orchard from which the Jhilpa man-eater was shot.

The camp at Jhilpa village continued. After three days of patient waiting, the leopard made a kill near Jhilpa village, but this time, it was a natural kill (not a human this time); a village pony. The animal was killed on the outskirts of the village, had dragged it into an orange orchard and had fed on it, mostly the hindquarters.

Overlooking the kill was a *machan* leaning against a large orange tree, supported by two poles. It was meant to be a watch-tower for farmers to save their orange crops from being ravaged by birds in the day-time and flying foxes (bats) late at night. This *machan* was in disuse, since it was the month of May, and well past the season for oranges. My father decided to use this for his vigil to sit up for the man-eater. He had that peculiar feeling which an experienced *shikari* has, when hunting big game, specially leopards and tigers; of meeting with success at last, for several reasons. From the pugmarks he could deduce that the leopard was a large male which the man-eater was reported to be; they also matched the pugmarks he had himself seen near the last two human kills; the pony was not a human kill; the leopard might disregard its natural caution and come back for a second feed, a natural instinct of the large carnivore. Finally, horse meat is known to be a delicacy for leopards and tigers. Thus, he felt sure that this leopard, even if it were a man-eater, would return to this particular kill.

The vigil was taken up early, in order, not to take any chances. Sitting up alone on a *machan* is a lonely vigil though very fulfilling and satisfying in some ways. Doubts of the panther not turning up fill the mind. But the dominant thought is an exciting expectancy and visions of the beautiful cat turning up from an unexpected direction. As night settles in with the *Chuck-a-Chuck-a-Chuck*, of the night jars call ushering in the darkness, a strange calm spread over the forest. As it grew dark there was an ominous silence in Jhilpa, some 50 mud and thatched huts scattered within about 1 km north of the *machan*.

The man eater of Jhilpa magnificent leopard about 8'6" between the pegs, near a record. Shot by my father in 1943, after he had made about 80 human kills the proud and brave villagers of Jhilpa are in the background my father took this picture.

The eerie silence of the forest was broken by a plaintive cry of a jackal from the far end of the orange grove, it was down wind from the kill and had probably scented it. The jackal kept calling and approaching, hoping to collect some more of its kind for a feast off the leopard kill. Pattering of small paws could be soon heard, circling the kill with an occasional *short yeoo-yeoo* and sharp yelps of the jackal. They were quite close to the kill and could probably smell the scent left behind by the leopard and were being wary. This was no ordinary dead animal but a kill of the dangerous cats. Inspite of the danger, the temptation was too great to resist, one of them darted in, snatched a quick morsel or two and scampered back. By now there were about three or four jackals and their feeding antics continued as they got bolder.

As about 11 p.m. from the wooded *nullah* side, far away, came the familiar *did-you-do-it*, *the-tee-did-you-do-it*, alarm call of the lapwing warning the world around, "danger is afoot, beware!" Although these birds often call even when alarmed by dogs, cats or smaller animals, but the intensity of its shrill call indicated something more dangerous and sinister than a cat or a dog was on the move; could be the man-eater?

After sitting on the *machan* for five hours, he was feeling quite cramped and wanted to stretch a bit. He was also sleepy and tired. Hearing the alarm call of the lapwing, he at once became alert and sat up with his rifle – (405 Winchester single barrel under level action), ready, his thumb on the torch switch. There was a scuffle and scampering of feet and then deathly silence, even the chirping of the crickets had stopped. It was the kind of silence, which sends a chill up one's spine.

Soon he heard the sound of some heavy animal below him. His right leg was hurting but he dared not move.

He kept stock still and in a few seconds the leopard was on it's kill and feeding. He let it feed for a few minutes, then slowly lifted his rifle, pointed it towards the kill and switched on the torch. The leopards tail was towards him and its head was inside the rib cage of the dead pony, he turned and looked directly into the beam. The heavy soft nose bullet took it just behind the shoulder blades and it lay still. It had hardly moved except for its tail flicking couple of times. Just to make sure he shot him one more time.

The end of the dreaded Jhilpa man-eater, ironically, was caused by its own fatal instinct of returning to its kill for a second feed; whereas it never returned to a human kill.

Before the Jhilpa man-eater was shot, three 'innocent' leopards were shot during the hunt for the man-eater. These unfortunate animals turned up in organised beats in likely places near kills the man-eater had made. The first leopard, which was shot as a result of mistaken identity, had a very tough time even after the poor fellow was dead. There were several people among the crowd, which had gathered to help in beating the underbrush where the man-eater was reportedly hiding, whose kith and kin had been killed by the man-eater. The 'innocent' leopard had finally dropped dead about two hundred yards from the spot my father shot it. Before he could reach the animal to check whether it was dead or not, some of the men among the beaters were so infuriated that they had already started beating it with sticks and poles and even the blunt edge of axes which villagers normally carry hurling abuse on it, "Take this you devil, you killed my wife", or "I will beat you to pulp, you scoundrel, you ate my only son".

The site was quite pathetic. It was only when my father personally intervened, they stopped beating the dead leopard. But their wrath was understandable. The irony of this incident was not lost on the local villagers for just two days after this incident, a human kill took place in a village 10 miles away from the place where they had beaten up the dead leopard. How can one be sure? One leopard looks quite similar to another, unless the animal has some distinct peculiarity, like being lame or some other disfiguration. This kind of identification is extremely difficult; particularly so when one gets only a fleeting glimpse of a moving animal and that too in poor light, as most human kills took place after sunset and before dawn.

As events turned out later, my father was not really sure when he shot this leopard, that he had actually shot the man-eater. He was only able to say so with certainly when no further human kills took place in the region. He had pursued the man-eating leopard of Jhilpa for over two years, in broken periods of weeks and sometimes months.

7

Haidar Mian-The Forest Wizard

(Kolash, Nanded 1950-51)

There was a beautiful remote forest block in the district of Nanded called Kailash. The block was named Kailash after a fort which still stood in the forest but was fully overgrown with grass, trees and creepers. It had been overtaken by the wilderness. In this block, there was a variety of game–from the tiger downwards in the pyramid of wild life. The most unforgettable character in this forest was however a human being – five feet nothing in height, named *Haidar-mian*. He was an ex-forest guard and now a fulltime *shikari* guide. He knew every nook and corner of the forest. He had an intimate knowledge of the habits of the animals of that small forest block, to an extent which was unfair to the animals of the place as events proved.

We arrived at the rest house in January 1951. Old *Haidar* was there to welcome us. He was standing in front of the rest house with his faithful old muzzle loader which was almost as tall as him. He greeted us with a broad smile. There were still a few hours of daylight so we asked *Haidar* if we could go out for something. He readily agreed and asked if we would like to shoot fish. "yes, fish", he said emphatically. We went along with the old *shikari* more to humour him than to get any fish. He took us a mile away from the *Dakbungalow* to a *nullah* with deep ponds and pools in it. He promptly climbed up a tree with a shot gun

A Singhara fish shot by *Haidar Mian*.

with a lethal ball cartridge and sat on a branch overlooking a deep pool. He kept watch at the water. After half an hour's wait, bang went his gun and he came down with a grin without speaking a word, he took off his clothes and jumped into the pool. He soon came up with a huge fish. A *singhara* fish with a flat head and a length definitely more than old *Haidar*. Its weight must have been between 60 to 70 lbs. half the head of the fish was smashed by the shot.

Next day, we asked *Haidar* if we could go for some bear. He readily agreed saying he knew just the place- near the old fort. We could easily go there after tying up the bait for a tiger (a buffalo calf) at the base of the hill, on top of which was the fort. We started early in the morning as we had quite a walk ahead of us. We tied a bait near the big *mahua* tree on which a *machan* had already been made.

We soon climbed up the hill and made our way towards the gate of the fort. We had hardly gone a few hundred yards when *Haidar* pointed out two black woolen ball like creatures passing us at a fast trot, they were a pair of sloth bear, one of them was much larger with a white V mark on its chest, it was a male and was bagged by my brother.

Our hunting trip that day had been a success. One thing that struck me about the bear was the absolutely clean and healthy shining black long hair (at least two to three inches long) of the animal. How it maintained it in this. After this we looked at *Haidar* with greater respect and realised he really knew the forest like the palm of his hand.

Next day, we wanted to go for a panther. *Haidar* promptly took us to a place near the foothills about four miles away and made a 'hide' next to a foot path coming out of the main forest, and quite matter of factly said, "*Sahib*, it is likely that a panther will come down this trail and maybe even a wild boar". Lo and behold! There it was. A beautiful large panther walked down the path barely half an hour later and stood stock still about ten feet away from the hide. It

I saw the tiger in the moon light walking away giving the bait and the tree we had the *machan* on a wide berth.

appeared so suddenly that we were taken by surprise. It stood stock still in front of us, looking the other way. I am sure it heard some slight sound from us which made it pause. My brother aimed and fired. The panther just leapt away and was gone. I couldn't believe that he had missed. We looked for it everywhere but we could not find it, though there were some blood stains on the bushes. We felt terrible. Now, we would have to follow the wounded animal to put him out of his misery.

Haider Mian.

Next day, we soon found the panther, rather, *Haidar* spotted it where it was lying; it was very close to the 'hide'. The soft nosed bullet of the high velocity rifle had gone right through it, just missing the heart. It had therefore walked zig zag for more than hundred yards or so and came back and finally collapsed barely 30 yards from where we had been sitting for him.

On our way back after locating the panther, a most curious thing happened. We had barely gone a few hundred yards when *Haidar* suddenly stopped, pointed ahead and whispered, "A wild boar–shoot". For the life of me I could not see it, surely that rock next to the path could not be a boar! At least 15 seconds passed, though they appeared more like 15 minutes, when I saw it. It moved when my brother from behind me fired. He missed it clean and we saw it disappear into the forest.

For the next four days there was no kill made by the tiger. *Haidar* was talking very seriously to my father explaining things to him, "*Sahib*, this tiger is a big *badmash*, It passed that way every day but did not touch the bait". *Haidar* said we should sit up for it. Accordingly, two of us sat up over the buffalo bait.

It was a moonlit night, but very cold and there was an eerie silence all around–one could smell and feel the presence of a tiger. I strained my eyes to see it but in vain. I heard a cracking sound- a huge animal stepped on some dried *sagwan* leaves–it was unmistakably a tiger. Five minutes later, some instinct made me turn my head to the left. I saw the tiger in the bright moon light padding away in full view of the tree where we were sitting, without making a sound. I could see that it had made a detour from the right side, avoiding and ignoring the bait completely. This was a clever tiger and knew what it was up to. I hope it lived up to a ripe old age in that delightful, isolated forest block. It had the last laugh against old *Haidar**, the forest 'wizard'.

*Haidar: *Though appeared at first as a comic figure, with his short stature and his oversized muzzle loading gun, was not only a master craftsman at his art of tracking wild game and his intimate knowledge of the forest-dwellers, he was a wonderful human being. Always cheerful and smiling; later we learnt of his sad passing away; having left behind wives and a brood of eight children. It was not quite clear as to how he died, it was either a wounded wild boar or some jungle accident which was the cause of his death.*

Grey or brown Partridge

8

Survival of the Fittest

(Nagaland and MP 1958-59)

The experience I am about to relate occurred when as a young officer, I joined my regiment during the height of the troubled days in Nagaland, in January, 1959. Operations against the hostile *Naga* rebels were quite a normal activity in the region.

Our Commander, a very imaginative type, had planned an operation named "Operation Savage". He had claimed quite dramatically, by getting down on his knees in the middle of the Sand model, in his exuberance, that he had planned to Crush the big camp and headquarters of Keto Sema, the then Commander-in-Chief of the underground *Nagas*. Being a young officer, the performance of the Brigade Commander at the Sand model seemed quite ludicrous to me as unlike others, I had a good knowledge of jungles. To crush a body of men in a jungle camp located in the heart of very thick jungles among hills, consisting of people adept in jungle lore, like the *Nagas*, was like asking for the moon.

In any case, being a young officer, in other words a greenhorn, I was given the task of establishing a block astride

A huge python in the *nullah* with a girth of eight to ten inches.

one of the escape routes of the hostiles. This location was in a place which was a paradise for all types of game including elephant, *gaur* (Indian bison), tiger and panther. Birds like the Imperial green pigeon and the great pied hornbills, were there in fair numbers. During our stay there, which lasted for about 45 days, I also saw a huge python which was at least eight to ten inches thick in girth and a beautiful but deadly King Cobra (a baby) which was about six feet long.

According to the original plan, this great operation was to last only eight days, so we had carried only eight days ration and provision but it actually carried on for over a month. This meant that our supplies had to be dropped from the air. We did get our supplies, but unfortunately we were short of rations for at least 15 days as due to bad weather the aeroplanes of the Air Force could be heard by us but no amount of coaxing or begging on the wireless would make them do a drop unless they saw us or our marked dropping zone. In this situation, we had to fend for ourselves as far as our rations were concerned. We were about 30 men, myself, one JCO (Junior Commissioned Officers) and 28 other ranks (soldiers). The boys being mainly *Rajputs* and *Brahmins* (from North India) were used to eating *chapatis*. We found enough stock of rice in the old *Kheti* huts which were left by the *Nagas* who had disappeared into the jungles when our forces arrived in the region. There was also an abundant supply of roots which were edible and other vegetables like pumpkins etc., in the *Jhoom Kheti* areas. This kind of food was on survival scale, put a lot of strain on the men and me.

Despite our best efforts, our Main Column could not reach the camp in time. When they finally did locate the camp, about 75 or more under ground *Nagas* and *Keto Sema* had made good their escape. He seemed to have vanished into thin air. As if this was not enough, the worst thing that happened was, that cut off from supplies of anti-malaria tablets and non-availability of DBP (a solution for anti-typhus use on clothing). Both these diseases were rampant in these parts. Some of the weakermen started falling sick in the forest itself. There was no way evacuating the sick. When finally we did get orders to move back to the base, out of 30 men there were about 10 who were already running a fever. They had either typhus or malaria. The remaining 20 also got fever within a month or so. I also got malaria after a month of my return from that beautiful place in the forest, where it was only the fittest can survive.

With our present lifestyle, we are quite soft for places like these, as our systems and bodies are not immune to such diseases like malaria and typhus. It is true when it is said that it was malaria which was the main reason for the defeat of the Japanese in Burma; there were four times more casualties caused by this disease as against battle casualties in the Japanese Army during their Burma campaign in the second great war.

These tropical diseases were so rampant in that area that even the locals were not immune from them, although their resistance was much greater. The medicines had a quicker and better effect on them as they had very little use for medicines due to their non-availability, unlike us.

9

Bilaspur Days

(Bilaspur, MP 1959-60)

In 1959, when I had been in the army for two years; my father, as a special gift to me, booked two blocks in the Bilaspur district of Madhya Pradesh.

The first halt we made was at a *Dakbungalow* near a small village called Dhoi. It was a small Baiga village. It consisted of about six huts and about the same number of families living there. One of the old Baigas from this village and his young son were guides during our stay there. The old man's name was *Karna* and his son was called *Choti*. These two used to work as a pair. *Karna* was old and his eye-sight and hearing were no longer keen. This handicap was made up by his son's keen eyes and acute hearing. However, *Karna*'s forte was the age old wisdom of the ways of the forest acquired through practical experience of years of hunting on foot with bow and arrow.

On the first day sitting in the *verandah* of the forest rest house, I saw a lovely sight–a racket tailed drongo catching some flying insects and returning to the same perch. The bird was on a *sal* tree, its branches were coming right upto to the *Dakbungalow*. It was a beautiful sight. Just then I was

Racket tailed drango among the *sal* trees near the *Dakbungalow*.

distracted by a *langoor* giving an alarm call some distance away. It meant only one thing, either a panther or tiger was around. Being so near to the village it was more likely to be a panther.

I quickly took my rifle and some ammunition, and asked *Karna* and *Choti* to come along. We soon reached the place from where the *langoor* was calling. I quickly made a plan of action and sat down next to a tree near a *nullah* and asked *Karna* to make a detour and come from the opposite direction. It might make the panther come towards me. The plan almost worked, but for the other monkeys giving away the presence of *Karna* and *Choti*. Their call alarmed the panther, which ran away before they could make an attempt to drive it in my direction, leaving behind a half-eaten monkey a little distance away from where I had taken up position.

On our way back I asked *Karna* to take me for a *ghoom* so that we could meet up with a good *sambhar* stag. He kept quiet for a while, then looked up and pointing towards the distant hills said, "we will have to go up there for the big ones". I was more than willing and told him so. He said that it would involve a whole day's march. I agreed and made plans to go there the next day.

We started early in the morning. We drove up to the foothills in a jeep, and then started our trek on foot. *Karna* and *Choti* soon picked up the trail of a big *sambhar*. I could hardly make out anything on the hard and rocky ground, but they kept following the tracks on the hard ground; an overturned stone here and a broken twig there, at one place a broken spider cobweb between some tall bushes, kept them on the trail. We reached a small plateau after climbing the steep hillside for about two hours. From there we made our way towards a depression in the ground where there was some water and around it wet mud. In the middle of the mud puddle a huge *sambhar* stag was sitting with most of its body completely submerged in the muddy water. *Karna* was

Sambhar **stag in a mud bath.**

very excitedly pointing towards the mud pond and urging me frantically to shoot. The *sambhar* was so perfectly camouflaged with the brown mud puddle around it that I could not see it; on hearing us, the stag turned its head towards us, it was due to the movement of the huge antlers that I saw him. On seeing us, it stood up and started to quickly move away. I took aim and fired. I saw the bullet hit the side of the stag. As there was a crust of dried mud on the *sambhar*, the bullet actually kicked up a bit of dust on impact. Following the blood trail it was apparent that the stag had been hard hit and through the lungs as there were bubbles in the blood. *Karna* and *Choti* followed it and quickly caught up with it. It was truly a huge animal and possessed a very good head. The huge *sambhar* after some difficulty was loaded on the trailer of a jeep, which was able to come up to the place by a circuitous route; we were back at the *Dhoi Dakbungalow* by sundown after a tiring day.

At the guest house there was news of a tiger kill awaiting us. After a quick meal and rest, I took off to see if I could sit over the kill, which was about 15 miles away from our location. On reaching the site of the kill, I found that the tiger had eaten most of the hindquarters of the cow. The pug-marks revealed that it was a big male tiger. There was no suitable tree in the vicinity of the kill, so I asked *Karna* to get a *machan* made by joining three or four *sal* saplings which would take my weight. I did not fancy falling down at the crucial moment. In spite of the difficulty *Karna* and *Choti* did a good job, but the perch was rather precarious and it swayed with the breeze, and at the slightest movement. I sat up all night and heard the unmistakable sound of the tiger moving about the kill but it did not come to the kill; most probably due to the makeshift *machan* on which I was sitting, he saw or sensed my presence.

Our next trip was to a place called *Tendu* which was famous for *gaur* (Indian bison) and wild buffalo at one time. We were driving from *Dhoi* to *Tendu* and had just come on to an open area in the forest. I could see a deserted hamlet with a few huts. It was about mid-day. Suddenly, a large pig crossed the road. There was something funny about this pig (I took it to be a domestic one because of the huts nearby.) A second look showed that it was a huge wild boar with peculiar markings on its body and it was moving at a steady trot without looking left or right. I quickly stopped the vehicle,

The tiger attacked the boar not realising what it was taking on.

snatched my rifle and some cartridges and ran towards a spot where I would be able to cut it off. I loaded up as I was moving and reached the place where it was heading for.

Sure enough it turned up there and when it was barely ten paces away, saw me and abruptly stopped, put down its head, grunted and charged me. Luckily, my shot hit him on the head and it just dropped in its tracks. The boar's peculiar colour was due to deep claw marks on its side, where, there were deep welts and pieces of skin and lard were hanging; on its throat were four, two inches deep tiger canine teeth wounds. It was obvious that the boar had been attacked and mortally wounded by a tiger, but had most probably killed or very badly wounded the tiger, which had dared to attack this mighty boar.

We could not follow the back trail of the boar to find the tiger but, the wild boar was so robust and had very thick winter lard (fat) on him, due to which the bleeding was very little. But one could well imagine and put together the sequence of events from the terrible wounds which the boar had on its body. Probably, the tiger was waiting in ambush on the jungle trail, on which the unsuspecting boar turned up. Not realising what it was taking on, the tiger attacked the boar (generally the tigers and panthers avoid large, single, wild boar). Once it had attacked the boar, the tiger sank its fangs into his throat, put its body weight on it and dug in its deadly claws on the body. The boar must have withstood this deadly assault and probably did not collapse under the weight of the tiger. The boar, it seemed stood its ground, dug in its feet and with a mighty effort must have shaken off its deadly burden. The tiger losing its grip on the boar, fell off; then the boar must have charged it again and again, cutting open the tigers soft under belly with the thrust and upper cut motion of its deadly bayonet like tushes. The tiger must have retaliated with its mighty club like paws, sharp teeth and claws, but with its belly cut open and entrails hanging out, it must have wanted to get away and crawled into some deep *nullah* in the forest to die a slow, lingering death.

I leave it to the reader to decide which animal was the victor in this clash of titans; because the boar even if I had not shot it, would have surely died from the grevious wounds inflicted by the tiger.

On reaching our destination, I regretted not having followed the boar's trail, as the beat was a blank one and the pug-marks of a tigress with two cubs were found; even if she had turned up, I would have never shot it.

Leopard

10

A Tiger in the Mines

(Baitul, MP 1959)

I had visited a place called Baitul (in Madhya Pradesh) well known for its old silver mines; my brother Ashok had also accompanied me. The mines had been abandoned by the owners as the quantity of the silver mined was very small and the overhead expenses very high and it was not profitable. These old mines were big holes in the ground with a maze of tunnels. Since they were in jungle, they attracted the big cats, tigers and panthers, particularly in the summers, as they provided a cool place to rest in (they were similar to natural caves).

We started the search of the mines in the hope of flushing out a tiger or panther at about 4 pm in the afternoon. By the time we had visited three of them, we were all convinced that there was nothing in them and it was too far-fetched a story to expect to find tigers or panthers there. We were now approaching the fourth one and were not ready for what happened next. There was a huge leopard sitting outside the mine and watching us curiously as if questioning us, "Hello what are you people doing here", before we could get ready and bring rifle to bear, he was off with a bound and smirk across his face.

Suddenly, there was a loud whoof sound and or a huge tiger came out from the cave.

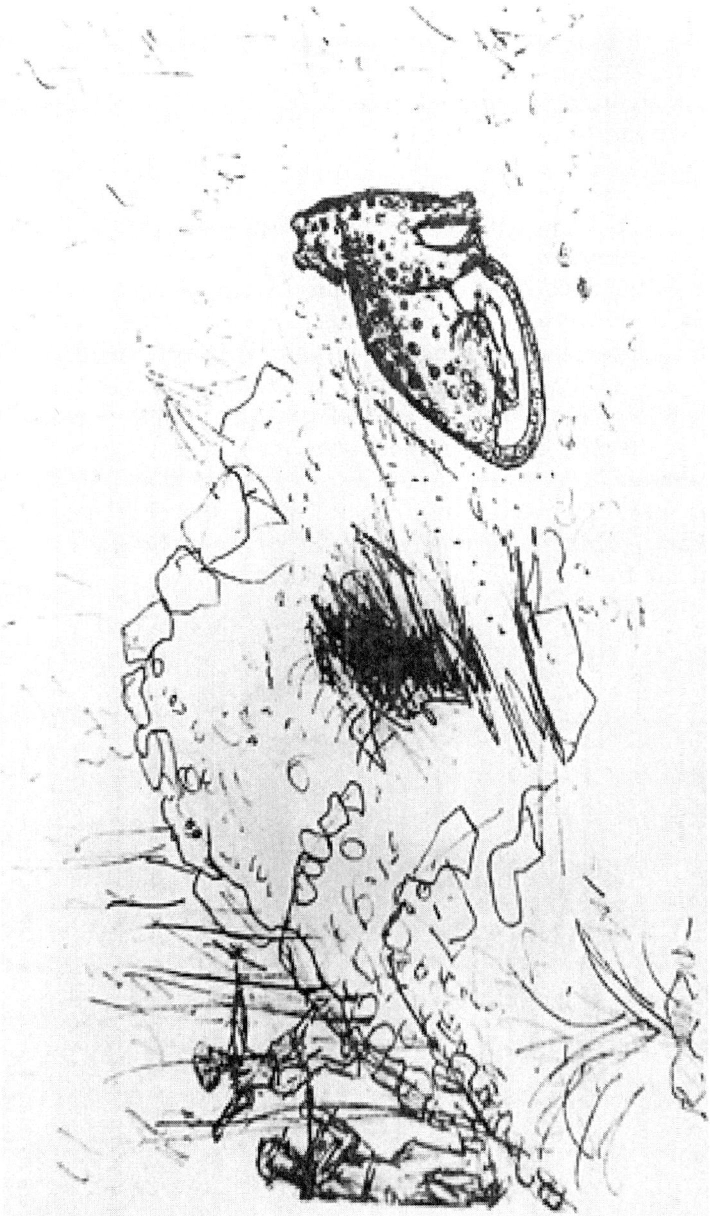

There was a leopard sitting outside the mine looking towards us.

There was two more mines to be explored. Now, there was a change in our attitude. As we approached them we were very quiet and full of expectancy but nothing expect a pair of hyenas, appeared from these. We had lost our chance.

My father narrated a story about limestone mine not very far from this region. Tigers were often found in these abandoned mines. On one occasion, one of the members of the hunting party got impatient and started saying that these local people were in a habit of exaggerating. How could one expect a tiger here. Saying this he caught one of the hanging roots and was about to step into the mine, when suddenly there was a loud, "Whoof"! Whoof! and a huge tiger came out from inside the mine, passed just a few feet away from this gentleman's legs and bounded away. It seemed as if it had a smile on its face rebuking in mock anger the children who had disturbed its afternoon siesta. This man who was at the mouth of the mine almost died of shock.

Black buck.

11

The Leopard in the Storm

(Baitul, MP 1960)

In May 1960, I booked a forest block in Baitul district in Madhya Pradesh. The forest was mainly bamboo, teak (sagwan) and sal trees. As usual after gaining local know how, we tied up buffalo bait for a tiger. Unlike other places we could not get a local shikari or guide, in spite of our best efforts.

For want of anything better to do and having no company, as my brother had to leave early to go back as his leave ended, I sat up on one of the baits. It was a bright moonlit night and visibility was quite good. At one stage I could hear the alarm call of *cheetal* from across the *nullah*. I came out from my hide and walked down to investigate. At night, no matter how good the visibility, the human eye can never compete with the cat's eye. As I approached the area from where the *cheetal* was calling, it abruptly stopped. In the morning when investigating, we found leopard pugmarks. I could make out where the *cheetal* had stood, stamped its foot in the ground and kept giving alarm calls till I came on the scene and disturbed it.

After three days a kill took place in the same area. The ground around the kill was so hard that it gave no indication

The *machan* was on the branch jutting out of the main tree and a bit precarious.

whether it was a tiger or a leopard which had made the kill. The hind portion of the cow had been eaten, which generally indicates a tiger, but a large jungle leopard also has the same habit.

A *machan* was set up on the nearest suitable tree. This was quite far off from the kill, being about 25 to 30 yards away. The kill was pegged down, so that it could not be easily moved. When I got on to the *machan*, I realised that it was set up on a branch jutting out towards the kill and not on the main trunk of the tree. This made it a bit precarious as the branch was not very strong. Under the circumstances and as the time was running out; I decided to let things be and sit up on the *machan* as it was. It soon became dark; though there was a full moon, there was no moonlight as the sky was covered with dark clouds. There was a slight breeze and the *machan* swayed with it.

After sometime, the gentle breeze slowly turned into a storm. There was a crash of thunder and lightning. Soon the rain was lashing down. My *machan* was swaying up and down like a seat on a giant wheel. It was about 9 O' clock at night, I had quite forgotten the kill and was concentrating on balancing myself in the *machan* so that I did not fall off. Suddenly, the storm abated and there was hush and calm all around. It was then that I heard the sound of a bone being crunched.

I focussed my eyes on the kill and immediately saw some movement near it. Pointing the rifle towards the kill, I switched on the light. There was nothing visible except the large carcass and rib cage of the cow; I kept the lights on, soon I saw a pair of eyes peering from behind the rib cage. I took careful aim just below the pair of gleaming eyes and squeezed the trigger. The bang of the rifle sounded louder due to the complete silence; but there was no other sound or movement near the kill. Nothing happened after the momentary blinding flash of the shot. I started imagining all sorts of things – had I really seen a pair of eyes or was it a figment of my imagination.

After waiting for a while, I decided to investigate. I got down as carefully as I could and went up to the kill, after throwing a fallen branch or two at it. I soon saw the leopard's tail stretching out behind the carcass; it's head still inside the ribcage of the cow and resting on its forepaw. It lay still and quite dead. Later I discovered that the soft nosed bullet had hit the leopard in the chest-traveled along the body and finally stopping near the tail. It was a fatal shot, it had not moved from its position as it had died instantly. Next morning one of my helpers reached the *machan* with a bullock cart, to fetch me and the leopard to the *Dakbungalow*.

The huge panther shot by the author. The Leopard in the Storm.

12

The Honeymoon Tiger

(Sarguja, MP 1964)

There was a time, when all good boys and girls got married before they were 30. In our case, my better-half was 24 and I was 27. I got married in January 1964 to a girl, who was not exactly wild about wild life or the outdoors, but did go along with my plan to combine our honeymoon with a jungle trip. I suggested this as a few days before an old colleague and friend of my father, who was collector at Ambikapur, also known as Sarguja, had written to my father to help him getting rid of a tiger in the district which had become a confirmed cattle lifter and was causing a lot of trouble to the villagers near a village called Dhindo.

The Dhindo forest block was booked for us in Sarguja, where there was a small forest *Dakbungalow*. The nearest railway station was 150 miles away, which added a lot to the unspoilt charm of this place.

The *Dakbungalow* was surrounded by beautiful *mahua* trees. The jungle just beyond was typical of Madhya Pradesh; sparse forest of *sagwan* (*teak*), *bamboo* and other mixed variety of trees with plenty of water in the *nullahs* in small

The authors wife Indu with a barking deer.

The Dakbungalow at Dhindo.

pools and puddles-water holes throughout the block. A typical *Madhya Pradesh* tiger habitat.

I had requisitioned a jeep, a driver and a local guide. The driver, Ranbir Singh, was a local, and was a driver by choice; a real proud Thakur (Rajput) by birth. He had done duty with the ex-Maharaja of Surguja and was an expert cross-country jeep driver. He was also very fond of his drinks and was able to imbibe large quantities of the local hooch without showing much apparent outward signs of having done so. Except for this weakness, he was an excellent man to have around in a place like Dhindo, due to his man-management and general expertise in managing the camp.

It was the month of February, 1964 there was still a sharp nip in the air. As we entered our block area, we saw a barking deer cross the road, ahead of our jeep. This was unusual as it was about 2 p.m. and generally animals are not up and

This snap was taken minutes after the Cheetal fell down about 10 yards away from us by my wife Indu, who was sitting with me on the ground for this beat.

about at this time of the day. Ranbir Singh immediately followed the animal into the forest in his jeep. I stopped him, in Ranbir's experience the shikaris he had guided did most of their shooting from a vehicle and that too at night, using a spotlight. (In my case I was only interested in taking still pictures of the animals with my camera).

Leaving the driver to re-orient his priorities I quickly got off the jeep and followed the barking deer into the forest. I soon spotted it and took a quick shot. It was a beautiful picture of a barking deer. The antlers measuring 6 to 8 inches. When I showed the pictures to Ranbir he made an observation. "Look Sahib, this first picture is a good luck sign and you will definitely get a tiger soon".

As we reached our destination some locals were waiting with the news of a tiger kill in a nearby village. After leaving Indu at the forest I.B., left immediately for the spot where the kill had been reported. We had no trouble finding the kill as there were two villagers already there, one of them being the owner of the dead cow. Unfortunately, these people had driven the tiger away from his kill by making a din and then dragged the kill for about 100 yards or so away from the jungle. From the pug marks, I could make out it was a fair sized male tiger. It was not going to come back to this kill for it had been disturbed just after it had started eating his meal. Bad news indeed. The silver lining however was that this tiger had made its last kill about four days earlier and would be hungry and must make another kill sometime very soon.

From the map of the block, I could make out the likely places this tiger would be hunting for his next meal. Accordingly, I obtained four buffalo calves, and had them tied up at the most likely places on the beat the tiger was probably going to be moving along. The strategy worked. On the third day of our stay at Dhindo news arrived of one our baits having been taken by the tiger. I decided to have a

A wild boar shot for the beatens (in the background) who had come in large number to beat for the tiger.

Thakur Ranbir Singh-The Driver, he was very fond of his drinks.

beat arranged the next day and give the tiger time to lie up undisturbed near about where the kill lay.

A *machan* had been made along the most likely route the tiger would take when the beat started. When I arrived at the spot, I found about 100 to 150 men had collected for the beat, including some folks who were there just to witness the '*tamasha*' of a tiger hakka or beat. After telling the beaters to keep absolutely silent, I moved off to inspect the scene around the kill. I was carrying my favourite weapon. .405 Winchester Rifle, my second weapon which was also loaded was being carried by a local named *Kalu*, a *Gond tribal* – an absolutely trustworthy forest man. On examining the pug marks, I found them to be of the same tiger which had been disturbed by the villagers and had left its kill on the earlier occasion.

A wild boar (one of two shot together) tied up in front of a jeep.

Indu his late wife and the Author taken by self-timer.

Just as I was looking at the half eaten kill and trying to make out from where the tiger had approached and attacked the unsuspecting bait, there was a loud 'bang' clearly the report of a rifle going off. I immediately realised what had happened. I also realised that this would ruin all my chances of getting the tiger as it was bound to have heard this loud sound too. I saw to my horror that there was a man lying in the *nullah*, clutching his right buttock which was bleeding profusely. There was a stranger, a village trader type, dressed in cleaner clothes as compared to the rest of the villagers around, holding the rifle with a stupid frightened expression on his face.

By then, I was quite furious and without a second thought gave this man a swift kick, snatched the rifle away from him.

The author and his late wife Indu (by Self timer).

The author (behind the tiger) with his bust missing : “I cut your face out of the picture for having shot such a beautiful animal, promise me you will not shoot another one in your life again” said Indu, who took this picture

A tight slap followed my kick. At first the villagers were aghast at this treatment meted out, but very soon they seemed very pleased and happy about it. I later learnt that this man was the local money-lender, who caused a lot of misery to the poor villagers as all money-lenders do. After giving them petty loans against their meager land holdings, he extracted exhorbitant rates of interest from these poor villagers. I told the money-lender in no uncertain terms what he should except from me if the tiger had abandoned my block due to his foolish action.

On examining the injured man, I breathed a sigh of relief. A minor flesh wound, caused by the thick sand of the *nullah* which had ricocheted from the bullet which thankfully had harmlessly dug into the sand, missing the man's thigh by a hair's breadth. I quickly gave the man first-aid- I always carried the kit in my bag.

**Haanka* or a Beat is an organised party of men who form a loose line keeping approximately 5-10 yards distance between each beater, depending upon how thick or dense the forest is, they move or walk through the said forest towards a particular direction; the idea is to drive the animal or the tiger in this case towards a place or spot where the *shikari* or hunter is sitting.

A few minutes later, I gave my instructions to the senior *shikari*. After giving me five minutes to reach my *machan*, he was to lead the beaters and start the beat without wasting any time. Another villager, who knew the location of the *machan* ran ahead, and I followed him at a run. We were half way to the *machan* when I heard the beat start with the beating of drums and loud shouts. I quickened my pace to reach the *machan* area before the tiger did! I was already breathing hard with the exertion of running when suddenly I heard the alarm call of a *langoor* monkey, which is an unmistakable signal that is given on seeing a tiger. I quickly got on to the *machan*, which was about 4 to 5 feet off the ground on a projecting tree on the *nullah* bank. Its location was ideal. It overlooked the *nullah* and a track coming down from the other bank of the *nullah*.

I must have been sitting in the *machan* for barely ten seconds when I saw the tiger coming down from the other bank of the *nullah* straight toward me. I carefully took aim, expecting it to go to the right or left, but the tiger just kept coming head on in my direction, head hung low, padding along, coming closer and closer. When it was about 20 paces away and almost about the same level with me, I nearly stopped breathing.

Such a beautiful animal, the very sight of which quickens the heart beat and never fails to have an awe-inspiring effect on all living beings when you see a tiger in the forest in all its magnificent glory, no matter how many times one has seen it before.

It was a lucky thing for the money-lender who had almost killed a man by accidentally firing off my gun, that the beat was a success. He was quite used to behaving in an arrogant manner with the villagers, mainly Gond tribals, as virtually every one of them was either indebted to him or would be requiring money from him. He had browbeaten poor *kalu* and had taken away the rifle from him. He was fiddling with the safety catch and succeeded in accidentally firing it. It was just providence that it was not directly pointed towards the crowd squatting in the *nullah* waiting to start the beat. I pretended that I was still angry with him and told him that I would have put him behind bars for attempted murder. He fell at my feet and was in tears. I continued to act harshly and told him to report to me the next day at the inspection bungalow. When he came the next day I made him sign a written statement admitting his guilt. I made him swear that he would never trouble the villagers again. If I heard of it, even after I had gone, I would institute legal action against him. After putting the fear of God in him, I let him go.

A blue bull or *neel gai*, the largest antelope found in India, this one shot by the Author in Dhindo, was almost six feet high at the shoulder and was blue/grey colour 1964.

Next day there was a beat for some meat for the beaters. I was amazed to see the number of animals in this apparently barren looking sparse jungle. During the day, we finally got a fine *cheetal* stag and two wild boars. This was enough for the villager's meat ration. Over and above this, they requested me for a couple of tins of *mahua* liquor, which I gladly gave them. During these beats, *Indu* also came along and happily sat on the ground and experienced the exciting proceedings first hand. She had been asking me on the way about what all animals were being there in these forests which could come out in the beat. I told her that since the beats were being conducted quite near by the village fields, a tiger was unlikely to be in the beat, but yes, a panther and maybe a sloth bear could be expected, adding that due to the occasional *mahua* tree and *ber* bushes in the area, both fruits being a favourite with bears; one or more could put in an appearance; along with of course other animals like the blue bull (*neel gai*), *sambhar*, *cheetal* and wild boar. I had given her all this information in quite a matter of fact way, not realising what effect it would have on her. During the beats when she sat next to me, she kept looking behind over her shoulder. sAt the time it appeared strange to me as to why she was doing that, as I had explained to her before the start of the beat, where to expect and look for the animals to appear, which was generally the area in front of us and not rear. As the beaters had come quite close and one could not talk for fear of disturbing and scaring any game coming in our direction, so I made a mental note of enquiring about it from her later.

During the next hour and a half there was a lot of excitement in seeing so many beautiful animals pass from so near us–specially one magnificent *cheetal* stag which came out trotting towards us, then sensing some things, it took a few tentative steps and stood stock still looking over his shoulders towards the oncoming beaters for about five seconds, barely three meters away from us from where we were sitting behind some cover. Later at the *Dakbungalow* during supper, I remembered about her strange-looking behind during the beat. She just shot back "Oh! You know, I was scared that a bear might come from behind", I was a bit startled by the answer and just smiled to myself, wondering about her not being scared of a leopard, wild boar or even a tiger but why a bear? This was our first outing in the forests and barely ten days after our marriage. On hindsight, thank God I didn't laugh or ridicule her in any way; as any married man knows that there is no answer to female logic – is there?

The author standing against the elephant, three elephants shot by him and his brother in Barkot block near Dehradun. See Chapter "Elephants Elephants"

13

Elephants, Elephants Everywhere

(Shimla, HP 1964)

In 1964, the District Collector and Divisional Forest Officer (DFO), Dehradun had issued special permits for shooting of a restricted number of elephants near Rishikesh in the Barkot block. This was done in order to drive them back to the Chilla Block. Normally, the elephants used to crossback across the Ganges – but this year they had not done so. The reason for this was not very clear; perhaps the elephants had become too numerous north of the river in the Chilla block, where these elephants were expected to cross over, as they did every year, before this. These elephants were now causing havoc in the sugar cane farms and other standing crops of the area.

A permit was given to me to shoot three elephants out of which one could be a tusker–I had to shoot three in all, two had to be females or *makhanas* (males without tusks). A royalty of Rs 200/- per elephant destroyed was to be paid later, as per the permit and confirmation by the authorities. I was also to inform the Dead Cattle Utilisation Officer to remove the carcasses, once the elephants were killed.

A stampede in the elephant herd.

When we finally left for *Barkot* for this unusual experience, accompanying me were my brother *Ashok*, a friend, Capt. *Susil Pillai* and *Nathu* a local guide and *shikari*. My brother's wife, *Usha* and my wife, *Indu*, also decided to accompany us. They thought it would be like a picnic. We arrived at the *Dak bungalow* after 45 minutes drive from Dehradun. While the ladies were arranging for the meals etc, with the *chowkidar*, we decided to take a *chakkar* of the forest looking for elephant signs. We saw a lot of footprints and elephant droppings everywhere but did not see any elephants that day. Despite our best efforts during the next five days, we failed to locate any elephants. On sixth day, we were following the tracks of the herd, when we suddenly heard some rifle shots, followed by the sound of animals crashing through the jungle. We soon realised that an elephant herd was stampeding in our direction. One of the other *shikaris* had fired on the herd and we happened to be in their path.

We quickly decided on a plan of action. We stood back to back next to a large tree. We soon heard the elephants rushing in our direction. We saw the herd. It appeared as if a wall was advancing on us. As the elephants came close to us, a large female, who was leading the herd realised that there was something wrong. She was barely 20 paces away and had smelt us. This female suddenly assumed a threatening and menacing manner. Panic was replaced by anger – she raised her trunk and advanced towards us. We let her come quite close and *Ashok* and I fired on her forehead hump from barely 10 yards. The shots seemed to have no impression on the huge beast, but it changed the direction of her charge with the impact and had almost gone past us, when Ashok shot her in the depression behind the ear. She crashed to the ground like a pole-axed tree. We shot at another female but without success. Soon the heard had disappeared into the forest. It was quite again. We had not seen any tusker so far.

After a few minutes I saw a movement to the right and saw a tusker moving silently in the same direction as the herd. I ran to cut him off. He did not suspect anything and I was able to get quite close to it. When I was hardly five yards away I fired on the depression behind its ear. The huge animal fell on its side but kept trying to get up. To my horror I discovered that I had run out of ammunition. I

Ashok and I stood back next to a tree with the elephants milling around us.

immediately ran for the other weapon. By the time I got back with the ammunition, there was no sign of the tusker where I had last seen him. On the ground there was a lot of blood. By this time *Ashok* and Sushil had joined me. We followed the blood trail but after some time it was difficult to do so, as there were too many elephant tracks and the bleeding had stopped. We decided to clear out from the area for a while.

We went off in another direction for about 500 yards and stayed away from that area for about 15 minutes. When we returned to the elephant which had fallen, we saw an amazing sight. Next to the huge female elephant lying on the ground, was a small baby elephant – hardly a few days old. It was about four feet high at the shoulders. Another female elephant was lying dead next to it and on one side was a tusker trying to make her get up on her feet. The tusker was also obviously badly wounded. We could see the blood streaking down its head. I quickly took a head shot and put it, out of its misery. All the three animals lay almost back to back in a heap, with the baby elephant standing next to them. We soon informed the forest officials about the three elephants which had been killed and baby elephant which was now separated from the herd.

In the afternoon, the officials of the Dead Cattle Utilisation Organisation took charge of the dead elephants. The baby elephant was adopted by a *Mahant* (Chief priest) of a *Math* in *Rishikesh*. I hope it is still alive, doing well and leading a useful life.

The author looking up at a bhoral sheep

14

The Ones That Got Away And Some That Did Not

(Dehradun, 1963-72)

Ever since I can remember, I had a deep love for the world of living things around us. My fascination with the flora and fauna began at an early age. The varied aspects of nature's beauty are to be found everywhere, if only one has the eye to see it. A strong sense of fair play and an imaginative urge to follow the rules of the game, to give as far as possible a sporting chance to the animal to get away. I loved the thrills of a stalk and the patient waiting over a kill on a machan, or just sitting up on a forest pool to observe the birds and animals coming to drink; one of my favourite things I did whenever we were in a forest block.

Harsil – 1963

It was in October 1963, that I was posted at Dehradun, when I got an invitation from the Commanding Officer of my old unit. They were located at a high altitude. There was a good chance of sighting *bharal* and ovis-ammon sheep, which had been seen in that area. I promptly took a week's leave and was there as soon as I was able to. I only had a week's leave immediately after arriving at the unit, I chalked

I saw a *bharal* (blue sheep) looking down at me from behind a rock on the crest of the hill behind me.

out a plan from the map, choosing the more remote and likely areas. I arranged for some snow tents, engaged a guide and some porters.

While the other preparations were going on, early next morning, I climbed up the hill overlooking the Unit area with ginger, my golden retriever, I had heard *chakor*- partridge calling when I arrived and they would provide some thrills watching them go zooming down the hill. Soon we were among the birds and they seemed everywhere.

The common *chakor* is a beautiful, colourful bird. They fly very sluggishly when flying diagonally past the hill side, but when they fly down hill, they really swoop and zig-zag at great speed. Ginger was enjoying himself flushing the birds that took cover in the bushes.

By the time I returned for breakfast, all the *bandobast* was complete and we moved out in the afternoon. We were a party of six; a young officer from the battalion, a JCC as a guide and three porters carrying the snow tents and provisions for four days and my dog ginger. We reached our base camp after one and a half day's march. We camped at an altitude of about 14,000 feet above sea level and the hill sides were mostly snow bound. The going was pretty rough and even a few steps taken in a hurry would make one pant for breath. So far we had only seen some snow cock (a large partridge like bird, and extremely shy). The snow cock would keep on going uphill as one climbed towards them, keeping a distance of about 75-100 yards from us, when they reached a suitable crest they just made a swoop down and down into the Valley hundreds of feet below like miniature rockets. The other animal we sighted was a Himalayan black bear; he was at a great distance and moved away fast.

We spent most of the following day looking for *bharal*, also known as the blue sheep. It is a very sure- footed mountain goat/sheep and is actually a cross between a goat and a sheep. It is much prized as a trophy because of the difficulties and the risks the sportsman has to face to even get to sight one of them. It was about 3 p.m., we were quite tried, as we had been climbing up the main range to a height of about 18,000 feet. I saw some movement on the skyline as I was nearing one of the shoulders of the mountain. I stopped and lay still. After a while, when I looked up, I saw a *bharal* looking over the rim of the escarpment and starting down at me. It was barely 15 yards from me, and only its head and neck were visible when it suddenly started running. When I rushed up the hill to see where it had disappeared, I saw it standing on a ledge about 20 feet below, after which there was a sheer drop of about 6,000 feet into a ravine from where another hill feature started. The ledge which jutted out from the mountain was just like a balcony.

It was a beautiful golden silk coloured *thar* (goat) and some ewes (female *thar*)

By this time, the guide had also fetched my camera. The *bharal* was a good-sized male and a good sprinter at this altitude. As I took the camera to take a picture of the *bharal*, and focussed on it, to my surprise it jumped up and moved off the ledge, around another rock and then disappeared from sight. All this I saw on the camera viewfinder. In the excitement, I didn't even press the shutter to take a picture of the *bharal*.

Instantly, I handed the guide my camera and followed the *bharal*. I found in front of me a sheer drop and from the rock face a very narrow and steep trail going over and around various rocks into which the *bharal* had disappeared. In the heat of the moment, I did a very fool-hardy thing. Instead of going back and finding another route to go down, I kept following the trail of the *bharal*. Before I realised what had happened, I reached a point after which there was only a sheer drop of thousands of feet. There was a loose shale under foot, I could find no foothold and started slipping down hill. I desperately clung to the small rocks on the mountain face. I used all my hill climbing skills learnt in the Nainital hills during my school days. Yet, it was of no avail. I just kept on sliding downwards, there being no solid rock to get a foot or hand hold. Those were moments of horror and panic and I really thought that this was the end.

The will to live is very strong. I desperately reached out for a jutting rock as I was sliding down. My fingers curled round it and the rock held, and my slide downhill was arrested. I lay there gathering my breath and wits; the *bharal* was forgotten in my desperate struggle for survival. I carefully inched my way to this small rock and prayed to God as I had never done before, to let it bear my weight. God was kind and the rock held firm. When I looked around I wondered how in the first place I had got to where I was! And now there seemed no way of getting back to where I started. One wrong step and it could be my last! By that time, the guide had come to a place well below where I was and could see me. A while later with his help and a lot of luck, I managed to inch my way to more solid ground, finally reaching the spot where he was standing. I told him what had happened. I was lucky to have got back alive.

We decided to call it a day as it was getting dark and planned to follow the *bharal* the next day. The whole of the next day we spent looking for the wounded *bharal*, but we could not find it. In a way, I was glad. And hoped that it was still alive. Later on, I was lucky to sight another *bharal* but its head was nowhere near as good as the one that got away.

***Maral Kanda* – 1971-72**

I was posted at *Simla* in 1971-72 and lived in *Chota Simla* a locality called Park Estate, named perhaps because of the elegant, tall *deodar* trees the place had. One of our neighbours was a Conservator of Forests, Himachal Pradesh. At his offer of booking a good shooting block for me, I booked a block called Maral Kanda. It was one of the most beautiful places I have ever visited. It was a small plateau at an average height of about 12,000 feet. This place had plenty of game, and also the elusive and rare *thar* goat which I wanted to bag as a trophy for my regimental mess.

Accompanying me was a local guide and two porters to carry the snow tents and provisions. We climbed up the very steep but wooded face of the feature called Maral Kanda. After reaching an area just short of the top, the guide said that we would have to leave the porters and our heavy baggage there and go down the sheer rock to get at the thar. After briefing the porters, the guide and I started climbing down the rock face. Initially, it did not seem so bad, but soon there was only sheer rock face and narrow game trails, mainly used by the thar. Anyhow, I doggedly kept following the guide with my rifle and binoculars slung around my neck. My hands had to be free in order to negotiate the sheer rock face. After about 45 minutes the guide froze and signalled me to come up near him. He had spotted a thar on another escarpment about 200 yards from where we were.

I took a closer look through the binoculars. It was indeed a beautiful golden silk coloured *thar* possessing a fine head. There was no way of approaching it without alarming the animal. So, I decided to take a shot from where we were. I lay down on a ledge, took careful aim and gently squeezed the trigger. There was a loud bang and I saw the bullet hit the rock about four feet away from the *thar*. I was puzzled because with this rifle I rarely missed my target. Anyway, the *thar* was also very obliging and it kept standing at the same spot. Perhaps it could not make out what the noise was and took it to be either a rockfall or thunder. There was no other explanation. I fired again. Another clean miss!

Now, I knew there was something wrong. I examined the foresight, and there it was, the foresight had got knocked out of line, probably on a rock. Well, that was that. The only weapon left now was a shot gun and buck shot, for which I would have to approach upto a range of 30-40 yards for an effective shot. I tried gamely for a shot all day. But the one with the golden coat was surrounded by its harem of several ewes which were very keen eyed and had acute hearing and were very difficult to approach. Finally, I had to be content with a young male which I shot mainly for meat, for the camp. With the rifle out of commission I shot some blood pheasant which were plentiful on the *Maral Kanda* plateau. I cut short my visit by two days to return home without collecting the elusive golden fleeced *thar*.

I have observed similar behaviour in wild animals when I shot wild boar among a sounder of pigs in a beat. One of them dropped. The boar next to the fallen pig kept standing, not sure which way to run. I shot one more pig before the rest ran away. I think, the animals were not able to make out as to where the sound came from, especially as I was using a high velocity rifle.

Kinwat – 1957

On my final vacation from the NDA at Kharakvasla before my last term in June 1957, I received a telegram from my father to join him and my elder brother Ashok. They were both going to the Kinwat Block in the Hoshangabad District of Madhya Pradesh. It was a block known for tiger and panther that were plentiful in that area.

On arrival at Kinwat, I was straight away taken to a place where I was to sit up for a panther over a goat tied as bait. I did sit up and had barely settled down in the *machan*, when the goat after being left alone in the forest started to bleat loudly. Soon it was dark and the sun was going down and a couple of red jungle fowl were informing everyone that they were safely perched on trees, and that every one should

A huge male tiger walking through tall grass looking towards its kill.

do the same! Next I heard the plaintive meowing of the peacocks and finally the chirping of nightjars and crickets. The goat was surrounded by dry leaves, so I was sure I would hear the panther before it got to the goat. Just then there was a rushing sound and a frantic bleat from the goat. The panther had come and killed the goat without making a sound, except for the last rush.

I aligned the rifle with the torch clamped on it and switched on the light. To my surprise, there was light but it formed a big circle, the centre was dark. I could not see a thing except for two green eyes faintly glowing in the rays of light, but the spotted skin of the panther perfectly blended with the yellow and brown dry leaves all around it. I could not make out where its body was. Before getting on to the *machan*, I had not checked the focussing of the torch. I quickly aimed at the faint glow which I presumed were the panthers eyes, moved the sight a bit higher and fired. After the blinding flash of the shot there was sound of the panther running away. After a while I could hear the night jungle sounds around me again.

Soon the head *shikari* came and after making sure from me that the panther was not anywhere near the tree where I was sitting up, came up and examined the place. He soon discovered the place where the soil was disturbed, the bullet had harmlessly got embedded there. The advantage of shooting with a rifle is if you miss, it's a clean miss, and this is exactly what had happened.

At Kinwat, there was never a dull moment. Next day a tiger had killed a cow about four miles from the *Dakbungalow* where we were camping. It was in the month of June, 1957. There was plenty of time before it got dark but these areas being quite remote, one could often find the tiger on its kill even during the day time.

We started for the place immediately. The party consisted of my brother, me, the head *shikari Topo* and two others. We made good time and reached the location at about 4 p.m. It was still very hot. Topo halted and told us in a whisper that the place was very near, so we should be ready. We approached a shady place near which was a pool of water in a dry nullah bed. There was a pin drop silence–the vultures were sitting up on the trees, a sure sign of the tiger being around. On reaching the pool we saw the wet pug marks of a large male tiger. He must have been sitting in the pool minutes before we arrived, to beat the heat of the day. Topo* put a finger to his lips and made a sign to follow him. He soon picked up the trail of the tiger. It led to the trees where the vultures were perched high on the trees looking down craning-stretching their long necks looking at the dead cow and the Tiger due to whose presence they were not able to start their feeding off the dead animal.

The vultures gave our presence away by flying away in alarm as we approached. We saw the tiger and the kill simultaneously. The tiger quickly moved away from the kill,

Five fully grown tigers in the wild, in the beam of the powerful light.

showing us its retreating back and tail. It was too fleeting a target to take a shot. Topo suggested that we could immediately sit up on a quickly constructed machan as the tiger would return soon. But we made one mistake and that was that we allowed Topo to drag the kill near where we were sitting. There was no other suitable tree close enough to the kill where we could sit up. The tiger turned up barely after an hour and I saw it clearly for about five seconds at a distance of about 60 yards, it was a magnificent sight seeing a large male tiger walking as if gliding through tall grass in all its glory with head slung low, it raised its head and turning it to look from above the grass, checking his motion a bit, looking at its kill. By the time I had it in my sights, it had disappeared. It had looked at the kill suspiciously and had not come close to it for it had been moved. I wish I had risked a shot. I had not realised that after coming so close, it would not come to the kill. However, it was a beautiful tiger and I was glad that it had got away. The lesson we learnt was never to alter the position of a tiger kill. A tiger is so cautious that it will never return to its kill if it has been disturbed or moved.

Adilabad – 1950

On another occasion, when we were at home for our winter vacations in 1950, my brother and I went out in an open jeep in Adilabad district of old Hyderabad Deccan. We were persuaded by some of my father's colleagues, in his absence, to go along with them, as they said it was only for a ride in the countryside, the only thing they would shoot were rabbits. Reluctantly, we went along. Being the youngest, I held the spotlight. We had barely gone four to five miles from Adilabad when I saw a pair of bright eyes, unmistakably that of a tiger. We soon saw three more pairs of eyes. Lo-and behold! There were five grown up tigers, together. They were obviously four grown up cubs with their mother. They all appeared to be of the same size. It was such a rare and beautiful sight that I could never forget it.

**Topo the head shikari was an old friend of my fathers; he was now getting on in age, about 50 years was fairly old for Gond tribals in those days. He was a man of few words; very knowledgeable of the Kinwat range; he had a jungle man's keen sense of knowing what was going on it the block –particularly about tiger movements; his network of villagers (informers, who lived in surrounding hamlets) was so good that he rarely made a mistake about tiger information and tying up of baits.*

In the early days after the liberation of *Hyderabad* State, a strange phenomenon was seen. There were a unusually large number of carnivores compared to herbivorous animals in the forests. Perhaps due to the easy availability of firearms for the local people, as no license was required, every second person had a fire arm and shot wild game for the pot, but no one hunted the tigers or leopards which were dangerous; perhaps it was just as well. Seeing those five fully grown tigers in the wild was an unforgettable sight, it was like seeing a circus show in the wild, and one of the most magnificent sights in the forests I had ever seen.

15

Outings in the Shiwaliks and Khadar of Ghaghra River

(Dehradun, 1963-64 &1975-76)

Some of the most pleasurable experiences of outings in the wild have been in and around Dehradun's Shiwalik hills and later on near Lucknow in the Ghagra river delta or Khadar as it is better known and recording all the game seen on each day spent in the bush.

When posted at Dehradun, I regularly took a permit from the forest authorities in winter months when one can spot birds and animals in the forests due to the cover being less. In winter the forests around Dehradun were full of small game; red jungle fowl, kaleege pheasant, grey partridge, black partridge and wild boar, barking deer and an occasional *sambhar* and *cheetal* herd.

My *modus operandi* was to go on a scooter early in the morning, with my Batman Gaj Singh, sitting behind on the pillion seat with my golden retriever, ginger in his lap. Gaj Singh, a Rajput, from Rajasthan could have modelled for a painting of a *Rajput* soldier. Tall about six feet, well-built with a pair of mustaches, to terrify anyone. Actually, this forbidding exterior hid a very gentle and gentlemanly person. He looked forward to these outings as much as I did. Ginger, though a golden retriever, he was by nature more like an Alsatian, a one- man dog; he was never more than three feet away from me if he could help it. When I got married, he tolerated my wife as a necessary nuisance! During the 1965 Pakistan war, after the cease-fire, he once ran across a mine-field in his eagerness to meet me. A few years later he showed remarkable patience when my young sons used him as a pillow. Ginger was so keen on going out into the jungle for these outings that he gladly bore the discomfort of travelling on a scooter in an uncomfortable position for an hour or some times even longer. As soon as I reached my destination, I would hide my scooter behind some bushes and then start my trek on foot. Once down on the ground, ginger was very good at flushing out birds from the thick lantana or *karonda* bushes, which I would never have seen or missed altogether if he had not been there. Being a 'gun dog ha' mostly went in the bush after game birds, mostly red jungle fowl, kaleege pheasant, grey partridge and an occasional black partridge. In this manner on an average Sunday round I used to sit and observe about 20 to 30 birds, during an outing in the woods. A hurried lunch and a sip of water from the water bottle was a welcome break during the *ghoom*, when I quickly jotted down the observations in the forests. Ginger, being a golden retriever, would never miss having a dip in the streams which had to be crossed and recrossed.

Once on a trip like this, ginger got particularly interested in a very thick patch in a sugar-cane field. Judging from the state of excitement, I thought maybe there were a large number of partridge or some other game birds in it. So, I quickly positioned myself on the other side of the field. I heard ginger growing, then barking and then with a loud yelp running for his life. When he broke cover, close behind him was a wild boar. Ginger was barely five paces from me; when I quickly picked up a stone, lying nearby, and threw it at the pig, which distracted him and saved ginger from certain injury, some cuts or bruises or even gashes which would have been caused by the wild boar had he caught up with him.

Ghaghra Khadar (1976-77)

I was posted in Lucknow in the seventies and one of the fish contractors of the Lucknow Military Hospital, Mohammad Hussain, came to my house, having heard from someone that I was a keen shikari. After a visit to the house his information was confirmed by the trophies he saw in the house. He seemed overjoyed and wanted me to visit their village in the Ghagra Nadi Khadar area, about 70 miles from Lucknow. He said all I had to do was to drive down to their village Sonepur where he was the headman, and be their guest.

I took him up on his offer and landed up at his place with a friend. I had been told that one could see, duck, partridge, wild boar, hog-deer, blue bull and even swamp deer. The last mentioned I did not believe till I actually saw them. There were plenty of fish in the river but one particular type of fish was very interesting to see as it jumped over the fisherman nets and used to actually fly or glide for at least 10-15 feet through the air; these fish were very sought after, we used to call them flying fish.

On the first visit, we arrived at Sonepur in the evening, so we just had dinner, that was *Muslim* cooking at its best; delightful curried fish, including tandoori flying fish, (described above), *sarson ka saag*, roomali roti and mixed vegetable pickle. Before we went off to sleep after making preparations for the morning *ghoom*. The next day Mohammad took us to the Ghagra River Delta to watch wild boar and hog-deer. Hog-deer can be pretty tricky. On this occasion, we were lucky for one came in our direction, took cover and sat like a partridge hiding itself.

It finally broke cover just as the beaters were on its head. The next thing we saw was a blue bull, it was a handsome tall specimen. As the village was primarily *a muslim* one, they were very happy to show us the plentiful blue bull in the area and wanted us to shoot some, as they were very destructive for their crops in the field, I did shoot one to oblige the villagers. They happily continued with the beat in another locality closeby where a big tusker wild boar came out with a real fierce look in his eyes; I was told that this boar had even killed one and had wounded many. I managed to get rid of this menace for the villagers, by shooting this wild boar while

Neel Gai in the forest.

it was rushing away. This confirmed in the eyes of the villagers, my abilities as a good shot.

On my third visit to Sonepur, my brother also accompanied me. Mohammad really looked after us and in the morning took us up river for about ten miles by boat. Then we walked about three miles. We reached an area which looked very good for small game and some other animals like blue bulls and wild boars. In the beat that followed we actually saw a herd of swamp deer. In the herd there were two stags with big antlers. How these rare deer species reached such an isolated area was quite a mystery as the closest reserved forest was miles away in the North. Anyway, the sight was a pleasant surprise. I hope they are still happily grazing in that area and have not been disturbed.

16

Wildlife! On the Pakistan Border

(Alhar, 1965)

After the cease-fire in September, 1965 war with Pakistan we found ourselves located about 25 miles inside the Pakistan border at a small railway station called Alhar. It was located on the main railway line between Chawinda and Sialkot. Both sides had dug down and there was an eyeball to eyeball confrontation at Alhar after the UNO officers arrived, one of them, a captain from New Zealand army, was a trouble-maker, who drew the ceasefire line in between the two rail tracks, one on our side and the other for Pakistan. But despite living in close proximity, we rarely had any trouble with our friends from across the border, except once.

I had anticipated the behaviour of our opponents, for that reason I had briefed my men that since we were so close (in range) from the enemy (Pakistanis), barely 100 to 150 yards away, we were not likely to have any trouble (firing of small arms) from them; but we must be prepared for the worst, because as was their nature, they were quite friendly and subdued immediately after declaration of the ceasefire, since after all we were about 25 miles inside their country, but as time passed, they would again become aggressive and do

The Author, at *Alhar* railway station (about 25 miles inside Pakistan, near Sialkot) just after the ceasefire of September 1965 war with Pakistan.

something to show it. In preparation for this eventuality, I had acquired two sniper rifles from the battalion stores and had set up two of my best marksmen as snipers', well-hidden and camouflaged on top of the Alhar railway station building (roof) which was in our possession. The high perch gave these snipers a big advantage of looking into the Pakistani Line of Control (LoC barely 150 yards away) in the flat terrain. The snipers were to "shoot to kill", to good effect at any machinegun fire from the Pakistani side. Sure enough, as anticipated, the belligerence from the Pakistani side in our area started after the eighth day of the ceasefire, they opened up unprovoked, heavy machinegun fire at night; my snipers were prepared for this eventuality, took their time, and placed three to four well-aimed shots from the point 303 sniper rifles, fitted with a telescope sight. Aiming just behind and below the muzzle flash of the Pakistani machinegun fire. They definitely found their mark as was desired, because the firing ceased immediately and it was never repeated by them again in this area for the month and a half, we were there in this area after this incident.

A few days after the ceasefire we had visitors (observers) from the various embassies at Delhi, these were Defence Attache; I can never forget the tongue in cheek remark of a British Brigadier, who on seeing the "Visit Murree, Visit Quetta", posters of Murree and Quetta, hill stations in Pakistan, on the dilapidated walls of the railway station building at Alhar station remarked "Join the Indian Army and see Pakistan......!".

As time passed, the empty villages and standing crops looked most desolate. In the winter (Nov./Dec. onwards) large flocks of starling arrived to feed on the standing wheat crops. These birds are called *tiliyars* in *Hindustan* and are not very good table birds. In the captured area I shot a hare or two and a blue bull.

Later we were moved-out to the border near *Shakargarh* in *Jammu* and *Kashmir*. In this area there was plenty of game including blue bull, wild boar, hog deer, porcupine, duck and partridge. On my regular rounds on the border, I often did some shooting for the table. Once when I shot some

Hog Deer .

mallard ducks in a stream right on the border; on the other side, one of the Pakistan militia boys in his *Salwar Kameez*, *majri* dress and bandolier slung across the chest (equivalent to our BSF) was watching me curiously as one or two birds fell in the water, which was no man's land. I calmly stood there and told one of my boys to go and get the birds, which he soon did. The militia boy just waved and moved on. *As-Salaam-Alaikum* sahib! I waved back and returned his greetings.

I noticed a peculiar thing in this area – the blue bulls used to keep on our side of the border (the *Hindus* do not eat its meat because of its name "*Neel Gai*") and the wild boars used to stay on the Pakistan side of the border (the

Musalmans do not touch pork). At night these animals crossed the border for feeding, "As on the other side of the fence the grass is (always/ or looks) greener".

What an irony of fate it was that these two armies facing each other could have been on the same side. One can only visualise and imagine how things would have been. We certainly would have been a much powerful country if we had remained undivided?

17

The Brow Antlered Deer

(Lungleh, Mizoram 1966-67)

The brow antlered deer are beautiful animals and are said to exist only in the Manipur marshes now. It was a pleasant surprise to discover them in Mizo hills near Lungleh. This was in 1967 when my unit was at Lungleh and I had to take a patrol to a place located a few miles from there. There was some heads of the deer put up on the inspection Bungalow walls, but no one could tell us about their history. I presumed that these must have been shot by the British officers (then posted at Lungleh) in Manipur. When I along with a two company plus strength of troops reached the village, we had to stockade the villagers as there were some Mizo hostile movements reported in the area.

Initially, the villagers were rather worried but later on when they were treated fairly by me and given some medical aid and surplus ration, they were very happy. In fact they took a delegation down to the local SDO (Sub-Division Officer) at Lungleh to make me stay there permanently! It was during my stay at this village that one day my interpreter brought a delegation of villagers who were keen to visit their *Jhoom kheti* site in the afternoon. Due to prevailing disturbance, no one was allowed to go to the fields after three or four p.m. in the afternoon. In any case, I was curious to know why they wished to go at this time. It was sometime before I realised what they desired. In one of the traps set up by the villagers, something had got trapped and they wished to bring that to the village. I at once got a platoon ready to go and investigate. The place was about two miles from the village. I had to be careful not to fall into a trap myself (nopun intended). On reaching the spot the village guide pointed towards the trees. Sure enough, a deer with one hind leg in the trap was hanging upside down from a stout sapling. It was quite still, obviously dead since sometime. I asked the villagers to get it down. When they brought it down, I saw it was a female *thamin* or brow antlered deer species. Its thin and pointed snout and splayed hoofs were unmistakable. The villagers that night had a great feast, but the meat was a bit high for me or my men's liking. I had a bit of it, in order not to offend the village elders.

From this experience it was obvious that the trophies in the inspection *Bungalow* were obtained locally. Some other rare animals and birds I saw in the Mizoram were a clouded leopard, a beautiful specimen. Caught in a steel trap by villagers, it used to raid their poultry frequently. But after it was trapped I came to know of it too late, by which time the animal had started rotting and could not be properly skinned. Once, I kept a lesser pied hornbill as a pet for a few days. It survived only for about two months but then it suddenly fell sick and died. I also saw peacock pheasants and the common Kaleege was quite numerous in its various shades from silver to black and blue velvet. The Red jungle fowl in its various shades of dark and light metallic orange colour, and the rare *bamboo* partridge had also made a comeback in numbers. The only good that had come out of the hostile activities by MNF (Mizo National Front) was that since all fire arms were impounded and the locals could not move about freely in the jungles, there was a natural curb on indiscriminate trapping and shooting indulged in by them earlier. There was a definite and noticeable increase in the wild game in that region by the time we came out of Mizoram after about two years stay.

A peculiar aspect of wild life in these parts of *Naga* and *Mizo* hills is that one never sees a crow or a vulture in the region. The reason is that not a scrap of meat is ever wasted. The people are very short of animal protein and as such what they can't eat, they preserve by hanging it over the fire. The

A deer with one hind leg in the trap was hanging up side down in the kheti.

only grouse I have against the people's attitude is that they just want to kill and eat anything that they can lay their hands on. Particularly, among the deer and birds; male, female, fawn–just anything would do in their book of rules.

18

The Dhol/Sone Kutta – The Wild Dog of India

(Mandla, MP)

Anyone who is familiar with the Indian forests and its fauna is aware of one of its most dreaded creatures – the Indian wild dog. It is known by various names like *dhol*, *Sone Kutta*; they generally hunt in packs which consist of five or ten dogs, sometimes large packs of up to fifty dogs have also been seen. It is the most ruthless killer and even tigers and leopards give them a wide berth, when in the same area. Stories of their killing game are legion; but the following story brings out the true measure of dread and awe the *dhol* is held in by jungle creatures, even by the leopards.

Once a leopard was chased by a pack of wild dogs and it finally climbed up a tree. Momentarily, it was safe from these marauders, as they cannot climb trees. The dogs kept sitting patiently under the tree. It was now a question of which of them got desperately hungry first. Either the dogs moved away first in search of other food or the leopard losing patience, jumped down and made a run for it. In most such cases dogs move away looking for other game. In this case they also did the same; but with a difference. One of the

Wild dogs eating a live *sambhar* fawn while the mother *sambhar* was watching helplessly.

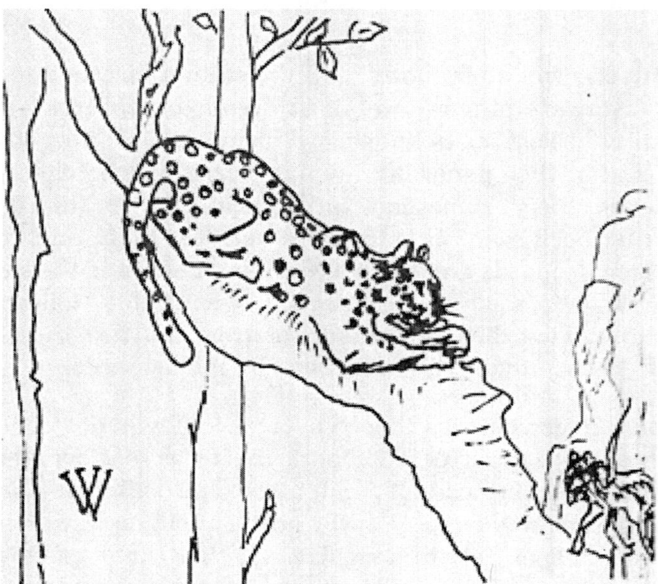

The dread of the wild dog (dhol) was so strong in the leopard that he perished on the tree, as the dead dog (dhol) was in the way when he wanted to climb down from the tree.

dogs had climbed a rock next to the tree and leaped towards the leopard. It missed the leopard, but impaled itself on a dry branch sticking out like a bayonet. This dead dog was in the path of the leopard whenever it wanted to climb down from the tree. Faced with this snarling dead dog on its way to freedom, the leopard's dread was so great that it is said to have died on the tree of starvation.

On another occasion, I saw a small pack of wild dogs eating a live fawn while its mother (*sambhar* hind) watched helplessly.

Indian wild dogs (Dhol) feeding on a *Sambhar* calf kill

19

The Rajasthan Experience

(Jaisalmer, Rajasthan 1981-84)

In Rajasthan, the real desert part of the Thar Desert is found in the Barmer and Jaisalmer areas. I had the good fortune of being posted here during my service career. Based at Barmer, my work took me to the wild areas of Pakistan/ India border in this sector.

The desert wild life is of a unique type. The great Indian bustard can be seen here, if one is lucky. The other birds are the common sand grouse, pin tailed sand grouse and the grey or brown partridge. During winter the winged visitors are the imperial sand grouse- a most delightful bird- and the lesser or **houbara** bustard, commonly known as the *tillor* by the locals. The latter was altogether a different kettle of fish as far as game birds went. Both the imperial sand grouse and the lesser bustard are visitors from central Asia during the winter i.e., from October to March when it is reasonably cold in the desert. The **houbara** bustard is the famous bird which the oil rich Sheikhs hunted with their hawks. The bird is very difficult to shoot as it has an uncanny ability to disappear in thin air. Its here one moment and gone the next. I had seen partridge use the ground before but I had

Houbara bustard : A winter visitor in the thar desert, a master of camouflage, hunted by the Arab Sheikhs (with falcons).

never seen such a master at the use of available ground cover as this bird.

I finally caught up on their tricks and tracked them by their footprints left on the sand. This was the only clue or

Chinkara gazelle being chased by banjara-hunting hound in the Thar desert.

tell-tail sign that gave away their presence. Once it took off, it carried on like a gull, dipping up and down for long distance even after landing it ran around quite a distance before settling down. Another comparatively easy way to hunt these birds was from camel back.

The other game in the desert are the *chinkara* or gazelle. It is very dainty and delicate looking animal; one can also see some desert hare in the areas where there are thorny bushes. Besides these game birds and animals, there are many birds of prey in the desert which prey mainly on rats, snakes and of course, other game bird.

Imperial Sand Grouse is a winter visitor in the *Thar* desert.

20

The Bird Sanctuary of Bharatpur

(Rajasthan, 1989-94)

The bird sanctuary at Bharatpur is one of the rare sites of the world, which has been declared to be a 'World Heritage' game park; that is, it should be protected and kept intact for humanity and not just the country where it is located.

The sanctuary attracts thousands of migratory birds, mainly geese of the graylag variety, pin tailed duck and mallard and many other species of duck and teal. Among the rare visitors are the Siberian crane for which it has become very famous. They used to come in large flocks, but now barely twenty or thirty come. I happened to see these graceful birds once from very close, during a visit to the sanctuary.

This sanctuary also has local animals like the blue bull, *cheetal*, *sambhar* and black buck, besides the wild boar. The sight of hundreds of villages cattle* in the sanctuary really spoils the visit to this place.

There is never a dull moment in the beautiful *kaladeo* Bird Sanctuary. If only one knows what to look for and where to find it. During the hottest months of summer, May, June, when the water ponds have shrunk one can see the amazing spectacle of flocks of painted stork, open bill stork, black headed stork, grey heron, snake bird, cormorant all frantically gorging themselves on the teaming fish in the scanty water and slush, where earlier there was deeper and plenty of water and it was not so easy to catch the fish. There are amazing incidents to watch like a stork catching a fish too large to swallow and the other birds chasing it to snatch the prize. In such cases either the fish falls back in the water due to ensuing scuffle or the bird manages to swallow the seemingly impossibly large fish, head first, down its elastic gullet, give a smart shake of its head and body, a earnest look around, and once again start fishing. The fish are so many that the water and slush seems to be alive with them. Fish are for the taking, and the birds seem to have an insatiable appetite for them and go on feeding on them mercilessly and endlessly.

*One of the directors of the bird sanctuary, a bold and positive Indian forest service officer in the 1990s, took a very bold and unusual step in that he rounded up these village cattle found inside the sanctuary and transported them in trucks to the Chambal Ravines and released them there; this positive step by him caused a lot of local political opposition, but he had the courage to persist with the right step he had taken. This immensely improved the sanctuary and gave great relief to the wildlife, rightful residents of this famous bird sanctuary at Bharatpur.

When the stork and heron are not fishing, they can be seen sitting on the shores and dry trees (babools) the cormorant and snake bird in their typical attitude of spread-out wings and tail feathers to dry in the sun; as if contemplating on the serious business of building a nest and raising a family. The survey and selection of nest sites takes place during July, August. The exact dates of building a nest, laying eggs and raising of chicks takes place between May to September and depends on the various factors like the timing of the monsoon and the amount of rains and consequently the availability of food for themselves and the

The Bharatpur bird sanctuary.

young ones. Generally, one can see the herons, paddy, birds, egrets and cormorants nesting in one colony during July and August. In late August and September one can see the multicoloured painted storks, snowy white cattle egrets, cormorants all nesting together. It is a perfect lesson to us humans the way the various species of birds build their nests and bring up their young next to each other in perfect harmony. The only disturbance or turbulence takes place in the nesting colony when a crow tries to steal an egg from a nest or a bird of prey flies past the nesting colony.

Other resident water birds one can see are the spot billed duck, the *nukta* or comb duck, whistling teal and the miniature goose like cotton teal. These water fowl are individual and shy breeders, some breed in tree hollows in the jungle or isolated places, particularly the nukta. One can rarely see these birds nesting but sometimes one can see them with their young in the water.

If you are observant enough, you may see the sarus crane on its nest and even the pheasant tailed *jakana* on its nest- floating on the water among the water lilies. Although birds are the main attraction of the *Kaladeo* Bird Sanctuary also known as *Ghana* (meaning many or large numbers in local language, obviously referring to the large flocks of migratory birds); there are several other variety of ground birds and other birds to be seen. Other animals and reptiles occasionally seen are porcupine, jackal, hare, lizard, python, cobra and a variety of water snakes, also leopard and even an occasional tiger has taken refuse in the sanctuary in recent times.

Bharatpur bird sanctuary revisited. The Siberian Crane Craze: "Eighteen (18) Siberian cranes only arrive at *Kaladeo* Bird Sanctuary during 1989/90". Five Siberian Cranes arrive at Kaladeo Bird Sanctuary in 1992/93 blazed the newspaper headlines (and of course no Siberian Cranes have arrived for the last few years).

The amount of publicity and importance given to this fact alone that the rare Siberian cranes visit the famous bird sanctuary every winter seems to have blanked out the simple truth that *Kaladeo* bird sanctuary is a naturalists paradise worth a visit any time or season of the year. It is because of its God given natural habitat and the fauna found in it, that it has been declared a "World Heritage" spot which is a rare and prestigious distinction.

Winter Visitors: The bird Sanctuary is already well-known for its winter migratory birds, mainly the water fowl which visit it every winter from November to February. The birds which make their presence felt by sheer numbers are the bar-headed and grey lag geese, duck and teal of various kind, like mallard, pintail, widgeon, pochard, showler and many others species. Other water birds are a variety of spine, stilt, coot, pelican and of course, not forgetting the much sought after Siberian crane.

But what about the hosts? The resident birds of the sanctuary present an equally beautiful and colourful presence at all time of the year if only one has the eye to see. These local birds are equally if not more beautiful to watch, indulging in various activities throughout the year.

Tail Piece: The bird sanctuary being one of the "World Heritage", locations, we as Indians, owe it to the rest of humanity to do our utmost to preserve it as it is and its natural beauty.

The local people of Bharatpur should also be made to feel the importance of this rare and delicate piece of real estate in their midst and participate to promote its preservation, thereby attracting more visitors and may be get some direct or indirect benefit from it. There are some obvious areas of developing local talent like making paper *mache* birds or even simple clay birds, painted true to life. These should be made with an eye on creating realism and those birds be made which are found in the sanctuary. Anyone with an artistic frame of mind and creative talent could take up this possibility which has a lot of scope for profit, provided high quality standards are ensured.

Siberian Crane.

Sarus crane.

Stilts and Snipe.

Grey Lag geese.

Grey Heron.

Painted Stork.

White Egret.

Shavls Duck.

21

The Boar which had Nine Lives

(Dehradun, 1999-2000)

A friend of mine has a beautiful farm, which is about 25 miles from Dehradun. My friend grows mainly sugar cane during the winter months. Sugar cane crop is followed by wheat, along with other legumes and lentils. All these crops attract a lot of wild life from the nearby forests. Prominent among these most destructive to the crops! in order of priority in their ability to cause damage to the crops are of course the elephant; just imagine the damage a small herd can cause to a farmer if they get inside the fields and are allowed to feed even for 30 minutes. Second, I would say are "*bandar log*!" the rufus or red faced monkeys. Third on the list are wild boar.

All wild life that now survives in our ill-protected reserved forests are protected under a blanket ban on legitimate *shikar* – which in my view has only a counter- productive and opposite effect of not being able to control poaching. The real sportsman of the old days was an effective check on poachers. Over and above the ban, the elephant and the red-faced monkeys even have religious sanction to cause as much damage as possible but no one dare say even boo to them! However, it must be said here that on my friends farm the forest authorities have helped by digging up an elephant trench around at least 2/3rd of the farm to prevent easy access of the pachyderms into the fields. However, the wild boar is an animal which is well-known to farmers all over the country which can never be stopped from entering the fields, particularly sugar cane fields to have their daily feed off it. To cut a long story short – there was this big loan boar with gleaming tusks, who used to enter one particular patch of sugar cane which was of a sweeter variety, *rasogulla*, as they call it in local farmer language, every night without exception, to have a good feed and depart during the early morning hours, when it was still dark.

The big wild boar used to go for the sugar cane patch in the farm during the night.

The talk in the party at my friends farm house one February night once again came down to the wiles of this big boar, who had got away scot free from various people who had tried to pot him – since a long time. My old *shikari* hackles were up and I, willingly, fell into the trap of trying to bag this wily pig. How wily and cunning he was I found out soon enough.

Once I took the task in hand, it had to be done in a methodical way. I arrived at the farm well ahead of the sitting up time in winter months (February) when it gets dark by 5.30 p.m. I spent a good two hours in the day light trying to see and locate his (the boars) foot prints-from which I wanted to see his regular route of coming in and going out from the sugar cane. It was soon clear to me that he followed no fixed routes on his daily visits. His area of ingress was so vast that it was impossible to say with any certainty that he would follow a certain route on either his way in or out of the sugar cane filed. It was also very obvious to me that the only way to sight him was to sit on his way in or out; because once he was inside the sugarcane – which was about 800 square yards – he was "king of all he surveyed". For survey, read all the sugar cane he wanted to munch, because he was quite safe in the sugar cane as it was very dense and as such he could never be seen or approached silently to have a shot at him. After a lot of discussion it was decided that a *machan* would be set up about 200 yards inside the farm boundary and about the same distance away from the sugar cane field – on an ambla tree next to a lantana thicket, approximately 50 yards, in the middle of the leechi orchard. It was agreed that I would sit up as soon it got dark and maintained my vigil till midnight. This place was selected as there was a lot of rooting about by wild boar in this area and it was possible that the old boar did visit this area either on his way in or out. I soon took up my position as decided- by 6:00 p.m. The moonlight was good enough to take a shot at close range; as I was told that this big wild boar, would bolt immediately on a flashlight being turned on. It was very cold sitting out on a winter night. As the evening progressed the human activity in the nearby village came to an end by about 8:30 p.m., even the *mandir pujari* in the nearby temple switched off the loud taped religious music. After this harsh, artificial sound, there was a sudden hush and soon the jungle atmosphere came alive. The roosting calls of the peacock and the red jungle fowl came from the nearby jungle and the soothing chik-a-chik-a of the nightjar could be heard. At about 9:30 p.m., the farm tractor went by, returning from some late errand. Barking of the local dogs around was a regular feature but there was no sound to remind one that humans were living in the close proximity. The wheat crop was sown in between the spaces or gaps among the rows of *leechi* tress, was about eight inches tall, it being mid-February. As the night advanced, it became progressively cold and with the heavy dew, it was intensely cold, I was frozen, trying to sit still. I always associated wild boar to being clever, having a keen eyesight and good nose and hearing; but I could not bring myself to believe that this boar had developed some special instinct and behaved more like a cat (a panther or a tiger) rather than a normal noisy, blundering, wild boar, I was soon to find out the truth.

It was now about fifteen minutes to midnight, the bitterness in the cold seemed a little less, when suddenly I heard a rustling sound from the bushes below and behind me in the lantana by some heavy animal. I was alert and ready for whatever it was. The rustling sound stopped as abruptly as it had started. I was staring into the space of the *leechi* trees next to the track on my right, not a sound nor any movement could be seen in the moonlit drenched short wheat crop in the space between the leechi trees, for the next five minutes there was no sound, the adrenaline, excitement started to get back to normal in my system, when suddenly intuition made me turn my head slowly and look to my left and there he was, the big boar standing barely 10 paces away from me, broadside. He had appeared as if from nowhere as I was expecting him on my right from the noises he had made in the bush. Only a cat could move so silently, but damn it, this was a pig, but then may be all those stories about this one having been brought by a panther foster mother could be true! All these thoughts flashed across my mind as I slowly brought up my weapon in line to take aim; avoiding any quick or sudden movement in order not to give myself away.

All this while the big fellow stood still as if sensing that some thing was wrong, I was about to take a shot, when suddenly there was a beam of flash light from the direction of the farm track and a human voice, calling out to me. In the twinkling of an eye he was gone, just vanished, just as suddenly and dramatically as he had appeared. The night watchman had decided to turn up at precisely the wrong moment to fetch me from the *machan*. This was the first sighting of this big boar by me. But the way he appeared and finally the way he was saved from being shot convinced me to some extent that not only was he cunning and wily–he was also being protected by providence. After having a try sitting up under the *leechi* trees and other places without success of even having a glimpse of the old boar – I again try to locate his movement going into and out of the sweet sugar cane patch. After one rainy night in early March; the next morning showed up the big boars hoof prints clearly. I found, he was favouring an approach along another hedgerow about five yards wide, running down the western boundary of the farm, dividing two fields. This hedgerow had a suitable tree to put up the small *machan*. The *machan* (a raised platform) was made for getting a better view of the area rather than the security it may provide. Finally, the *machan* was put up in a clump of trees located midway in the hedgerow about 70 yards down the farm boundary. After having sat up after dark and after all the normal human noises had ceased, I was pleasantly surprised by a night jar, who came and sat on a tree stump barely three feet away from my head as I sat stock still on the *machan*. The night jar glared at me with his large owl like eyes clearly visible to me in the bright moon light, as if to say – Hello! Where did you come from and what are you doing here? But when I made no move to disturb him, he kept on sitting for a while probably having decided that I was after all a tree stump. This incident proved at least one thing that my perch on the tree was well-camouflaged and I was sitting motionless; as all wild things that move under the cover of darkness to feed have a very keen eyesight and acute hearing and are able to detect any movement or sound. At about 8:45 p.m. I had my second glimpse of the old boar. Instead of coming in along the lantana hedgerow, as expected , he was cutting across the half grown wheat fields diagonally towards the sugar cane about 80 yards away. He was moving silently as was his habit and I saw him in the moonlight because of a clik-clik sound sometimes made by big wild boar, clamping on their tusks involuntarily; this time I did not shoot because he was too far for a shot in the dark, as even in the bright moonlight the foresight could not be seen.

After a few days, when I tried sitting up for the old boar again, we had again shifted the *machan* position to a small tree at the eastern end of the lantana hedgerow – hoping that in this way I may see him at a closer range. It worked, he crossed the wheat field more or less on the same path as when I saw him last. This time he was about 25 – 30 yards. I quickly had him in my sight and pressed the trigger, instead of the beam of the heavy rifle, there was a dull click, I pressed the second trigger (as it was a double barrel rifle borrowed from my host), another click, I could not believe it, both the shots were misfires. This again brought out the fact that his time had just not come. He was just too lucky and not only uncannily clever.

The old boar's timings of coming into the farm (sugar cane patch) and going out of it were now fairly well- estimated. His time for leaving the sugar cane and the farm after the night feed was about four and five a.m.; when it was still quite dark and the human movements and activity had not started. Even the over enthusiastic *pandit* in the village temple switched on his tape recorder only about 6:00 in the morning. This time, I decided to sit up at about 3:30 a.m. in the morning, to try and have a shot at him on his onwards trek from the sugar cane. The alarm clock didn't go off and I did not wake up in time to go and sit up. When I woke up it was 5:45 a.m. and bright day light outside. It was too late for the boar (so I thought) but I decided to go out for a walk and meet Surat Singh*, the night watchman.

On my way out I took my shotgun along just in case old porky was still around; when I was out of the farmhouse on the track running North-South along the sugar cane field, I saw a milkman coming up the track on his cycle balancing two huge milk cans on either side, heading for the village. I heard the loud devotional songs which started to play on the temple loud speaker. I least expected the big boar to still be around, but what do I see, the boar trotting across the track just from behind where the man with the milk cans was coming towards me. It was six a.m. and bright day light, he even stopped for two seconds or so to throw a quick glance at me, as if to say "Hello there old chap! see you again next time", and continued his trot towards the jungle, he was more than about 100 yards away, clearly out of the twelve bore range. That was the fourth time and last time I saw him alive, he certainly had the last laugh any way so far. It was to be seen, if he had the proverbial 'nine lives like the cats'; which meant I had to sight him five more times!

***Surat Singh** a very loveable and robust watchman employed by my friend on his farm, was an ex-jawan from the BSF, he has a very friendly and good nature and had qualities of patience like in a good *shikari*, and was a very good tracker. He soon after the above incident (barley 10 days) took a long shot in the moonlit night, about 150 to 200 yards distant, (with my friend's rifle, which he carried sometimes during his duties) at the boar and succeeded in bagging him.

22

Some Thoughts on Wildlife Protection

The great English Noble Laureate Sir Bertrand Russell in his book "*How to Achieve Happiness*" had commented on the subject of hunting, as being **one of man's oldest and most deeply satisfying hobbies** and the instinct is present in most men in a dormant state. This instinct maybe indulged in now also with a difference – changing the killing part to photographing instead. Exchange the rifle for a camera.

After Independence particularly, the implementation of game laws has been very lax or non-existent. The main aim of the Forest Department was to look after the forests. But that is a loaded question – who was looking after whom! The beginning of the end was with the advent of second hand jeeps (cross country capability) and weapons after the war, so that the spot light *shikari* who paid little or no attention to what he shot – male, female or a fawn, the important thing was to shoot something, which was blinded in the spot light. Besides these poachers, the main culprit in reducing the game or wild life in the country has been the uncontrolled felling of forest trees, and population growth which is unchecked and has a direct bearing on actually clearing forest land for agriculture in an agro- based economy like ours, in other words rampant encroachment on wild life habitat.

In my opinion it is still possible to raise game artificially or protect the animals in the restricted areas and earn foreign exchange by controlled permit system. This method can be worked out and implemented as a forest-based industry. This also will give employment to the locals of the forests who have the know-how. Birds like partridge, quail and red jungle, fowl and kaleege pheasants can be bred like in England, USA and Canada which are later set free in the wild and hunting allowed in a restricted area, at a price by those who can afford it; **it cannot be a common man's sport.**

It is an amazing fact that the vast majority of the people, who are conservationists are all ex-*shikaris* or hunters. They were hunters primarily due to the thrill and pleasure derived from being in the wild environment and the pleasure they got simply looking at wild life in all its glory. The things done under the garb of sport like the famous Bharatpur duck shoots were ugly extravaganzas by people, who did not know better. Like an ex- *Maharajah* being proud of having shot more than 500 tigers; even his *shikar* tents were made of tigers skins, which truly was in very bad taste to say the least. But such aberrations only prove the rule that the vast majority of the sportsmen who indulged in this hobby would be ready to help to do anything to preserve this great heritage of our country. More scientific studies should be made to ensure the survival of our species like the *gir* lion, snow leopard and introduction of the Asiatic Cheetah now extinct. The Asiatic lions found in the *gir* also require fresh induction of lions from outside, in order to improve the breed and prevent too much of in breeding. Hunting farms could be leased out to the people who have ability to run such places; these could become foreign exchange earners.

However, these projects will require Government approval but will have to be run privately. This will keep the local people usefully employed. It will also provide the Government with readymade machinery for prevention of poaching and illegal hunting. For the success of the environmental crusade and to put an end to poaching it is most essential that the local people are involved.

The self-appointed guardians of environment and ecology in India are people who do so for political reasons and have very little real commitment to this important task. They lack in depth knowledge of the subject. With some it is a passing fancy or a fad as it is fashionable to be espousing a cause to be kind to animals.

Where as ecology and environment is a very vast and serious subject which should take priority in all walks of life in a developing country like ours. On this subject there is a need for co-ordinated effort in the agriculture, forest and environment ministries and the ministry of industries. Any development not paying heed to local ecology can cause a disaster to the environment. The industry which pollutes the atmosphere or pours down poison into rivers will kill all living things in it.

A farmer today should not be allowed to hunt or trap game in the name of protecting his crops; he may be compensated by other means. It is very essential that this should be strictly enforced.

Our growing unchecked human population is definitely the main factor behind our ecological imbalance and problems. Land which was barren, overgrown by shrubs, which gave shelter to many animals and living things has been brought under the plough and wildlife has been elbowed out. This means that we must wake up and take notice and try and stop the increase in population on a war-footing (like China) as it puts a heavy pressure on the environment and ecology and pushes it on a headlong rush towards disaster.

We can make a small beginning by planting suitable trees in the areas, which have been denuded of forests. Plantations also should be undertaken to provide fodder for the animals and fuel for burning.

Unless these things are looked into and a political will is shown by concerned authority and the leaders of the country to protect our forests and wildlife at all costs, unless the forests will soon disappear altogether and with the forests the animals and that inhabit it.

23

Some Suggestions for Protection of the Tigers

The fact that tigers are not safe in our tiger reserves, is no sudden discovery.

1. Suggestions:

A. ***Set a thief to catch a thief:*** In and around the tiger reserves the hardcore poachers and trackers, who are at present being used by the nefarious "big fish" dealers in tiger products, and causing the disappearance of tigers, must be sought after and employed by the tiger project and be included in the protection force; pay them three time the *sal*ary of a forest ranger, look after his family needs by providing him the best house in the village, thereby elevating his prestige from a shadowy poacher to a honourable tiger protector.

B. ***Intelligence about the tigers in the tiger reserves at all times***: Intelligence in tiger protection is of paramount importance, this can be achieved by having the right type of person employed inside the tiger reserves and also in key locations around the tiger reserves, in restaurants, guest houses, taxi drivers, *chowkidars* of government guest houses inside the tiger reserves, *mahavats* of elephants working inside the reserves, contractors and the staff of canteens, cafeterias

A Huge Tiger in the Kanha Reserve – February 1945.

etc., inside the reserves are all likely conduits for information about tigers to the villains (the ones who are after the tigers). The tables should be turned on getting information about the people who are after the tigers from the above named conduits, by employing them as our own intelligence agents. The other aspect of tiger intelligence is to know at all times as to how many tigers and their approximate locations, sex, size, etc., are in the reserve at any given time. This is not a difficult thing for the people who live in tiger habitats, if used by the forest department in a positive relationship with them.

C. ***Education of villagers in and around tiger reserves.*** Besides physically stopping the cattle from entering the tiger reserves by setting up electric fence, digging ditches etc; it will be of benefit to try and educate the local villagers in the benefits of :

(i) **Stall feeding of animals,** cows, buffaloes and goats.

(ii) **Growing of certain fast growing fodder plants** in and around the vicinity of the village.

(iii) **Improving of the breed of cattle by government** veterinary support (artificial insemination etc).

(iv) Inculde the **benefits of protecting the tiger to the villagers,** in local school curriculums; how they as future citizens will benefit if the tiger is preserved.

Note: Ensure employment of maximum villagers/tribals from the vicinity of the tiger reserves in the protection force, but ensure that they are good trackers and jungle-men; even if they are not good trackers, these people living in and around forest can be quickly trained to become good at this job/task. This aspect is most important because at present only lip service is being given to the fact that the people who are most affected in the area should reap the benefits of protecting the tiger.

D. ***Elite killing force in the killing zone:*** It should be common knowledge in and around the tiger reserve, that anybody found inside the tiger reserve maybe shot on site. This fact should be loudly proclaimed by means of putting up posters, by word of mouth and notices at suitable locations, this information should be effectively spread in the countryside around the tiger reserve.

But in order to enforce such wishful thinking we must have proper legislation to empower an elite tiger protection force drawn from among the best volunteers from Forest Department, Police, Army, to shoot to kill anyone found inside the tiger reserve where he is not supposed to be. This ruthless action against the poachers is most essential even at the risk of loss of some innocent villagers etc. It has to be remembered that the poacher himself will never hesitate to kill any forest ranger or guard when in danger of being detected or caught.

E. ***The latest equipment and gadgets to the elite force***: Although the saying that it is not the weapon but the man behind the weapon which counts; but in modern day parlance it will go a long way in raising the morale of the tiger protection force if they are provided with the latest gadgets available to do their job – the best weapons and night vision devices, the best cell phones and communication systems, the best vehicles for fast and efficient movement

Durga Maa Ka Shikar.

inside and around the tiger reserves, micro-light aircraft, helicopter support from the nearest Air force/ Army base. It should be ensured that this force is put through rigorous training for the job at hand and a continuous training program be incorporated in their duties. The job of vigilance of this type will not be easy, qualities like dedication and loyalty to the team will be of paramount importance to the ultimate success of this protection force and its ability to protect the tiger.

Tailpiece

Protecting the tiger in India in the habitat where they have so far survived inspite of so many problems, like overwhelming human encroachment, is not going to be easy; it will require political will, a guided effort by experts at protection of the subject (tiger) with no personal agenda or axe to grind. Finally, it will cost a lot of money? But to save the tiger we must – even if it is worth all the gold in India – make an honest effort to protect the mighty tiger; otherwise who knows we may even greatly upset *Durga Maa* if we fail to protect the tiger, after all the tiger has been her vehicle on which she rides out to crush all evil!!

Jungle Sketch Book
And
Vintage Photographs

"Lady", the authors half-breed Spaniel, at Halflong lake, (near Nagaland) in October 1959. Halflong famous for its oranges, is better known for 'Jatinga', a village nearby where ornithologists the world over are not sure why a varied species of birds including migratory birds (mallards, pintail ducks etc.) almost commit 'Harakiri'. These birds loose all sense of direction and sit on the ground in a daze or fly half-heartedly about in the fog where the villagers using either hand held torches or artificial gaslights to attract the birds and club them to death in large numbers quite easily. Halflong was also a rest and recreation camp for the American and allied troops during the Second World War in 1944-45 (Burma campaign against the Japanese invaders). See Chapter "Survival of the Fittest".

In the center, my father (Late Mr N.S. Verma), shot these two tigers on the same kill who turned up within a gap of two hours on the same night. He thought he fired on the same tiger, they were both fully grown male tigers. Chanda district, Old C.P. now M.P. May 1935. Flanked by Kallu his *shikari* or tracker, turban on his head and driver, Mohammed.

Family of grey or brown partridges. See Chapter : "The Rajasthan Experience"

Crows on dry tree on a rainy day. See Chapter "Jungle Sketch Book"

A tigeress is very protective and dangerous when she is with her cubs.

Black buck See Chapter "Jungle Sketch Book".

A *Cheetal* herd See Chapter "Jungle Sketch Book".

The big tiger sniffed and circled the car at dead of night, before going away into the forest*

***Our father left the two of us in the car (myself age eight and my brother age ten) locked in the car, after the clutch plate of the car packed up in a *nullah*, while returning to Mandala from Kanha Kesli (now Kanha National Tiger Reserve in *Madhya Pradesh*) to get help from a village 10 miles away in January 1946. A very big tiger visited us during the night; we only discovered this' when we got out of the car in the morning, from the pug marks all around the car in the wet sand, they were huge about the size of a common dining plate.**

A typical leopard attack on *langoor* monkeys on a tree for making a kill :

(1) Leopard watching some *langoors* closely, isolated on a clump of low trees.

(2) Leopard charges the trees, aiming for the closest *langoor*.

(3) Leopard takes a leap on the tree, the *langoors* panics and jumps/ falls down to the ground.

(4) Leopard does not climb the tree but quickly leaps down on the monkey on the ground and grabs the kill.
Note: The three and four motions of the leopard are made in one fluid movement which ends in the leopard making the kill.
See Chapter "Jungle Sketch Book"

Indian wild buffalo Kaziranga National Park. See Chapter "Jungle Sketch Book".

Indian one-horned rhino's in Kaziranga wildlife sanctuary in Assam, India. See Chapter "Jungle Sketch Book".

A group of Hill Langoor Monkeys near Mussoorie.

The author standing against the elephant, three elephants shot by him and his brother in Barkot block near Dehradun. See Chapter "Elephants Elephants"

The author in the centre flanked by his wife Indu on the right and on the left is Maharaj Gaj Singh of Jodhpur.

Indu (my late wife) and my younger son, Arun in Barmer Bazar (Rajasthan), December 1981. See "Dedication".

24

KHATAWLI

(A paradise for wildlife - 1953)

Khathawli, with *its* abundance of flora and fauna and a small but comfortable *Dak Bungalow* was a real paradise on earth.

Khatawli is a small *village about* 50 *miles.* from Katni (famous for its cement factory) in *Jabalpur* district. The route from *Katni* to *Khatawli* was *mostly* an *unmettaled* road and had to be undertaken on bullock carts; a factor, which discouraged most visitors. The un-bridged *Ram Ganga* River

Khatauli Dak Bunglow

which was quite deep and *could* be crossed on foot and by carts only at the ford sites, and was also known for its man eating crocodiles which was also a big deterrent to people wanting to visit *Khatawli.*

The forest *Dak bungalow* was located near the lake. It was well furnished and barely half a km. from the *Khathawli* forest block. The block itself was full of big and small game. There was always a resident tiger in the block, besides other animals, panther, *sambhar, cheetal* and wild boar in fairly large numbers. In winter months flocks of grey lag geese and other water fowl could be seen in the lake nearby.

On our arrival at the forest bungalow We were welcomed by the local forest ranger who was expecting us. This was in accordance with the custom in those days which helped the visitor who had booked the block as the ranger kept the District Forest Officer and other officials informed about all .the activity in the reserved forest. The forest ranger kept a record of the game shot by the visitor. He kept a strict check that no female deer or out of season bird was shot- only the pennitted numbers were shot and the royalty paid for the same. The sportsman in tum reported any poacher or unauthorized felling of trees, ifhe noticed any during his visit and stay at the block. This relationship between the pUblic and the forest officials Was a very healthy one and unfortunately fell into disuse OVer the last 30 years or so due to which all bad practices have crept in, like rampant poaching and illegal felling of trees. Since the legitimate *shikaris* or sportsmen were stopped in the name of game preservation, from entering the reserved forest, there was no transparency left in the action of those who were the guardians of the forest.

Old Matru soon came to meet us after the forest ranger left, *Matru* was rather tall for a *Gond* tribal, he like most of his tribe Was a very good tracker, keen eyed and had a real feel for the forest. Above all he knew *Khatawli* like the palm of his hand. Surprisingly he was also a good organizer of beats *(hankas)* and in managing the camp. He had been my father's *shikari* and tracker for the last 30 years or more and had been seeing us as small boys. Looking at him now, one could not quite guess his age. He was still very fit but the only thing that compelled him to keep a helper now was his failing eyesight. His age must have been about 55 years (which was very old for villagers in those days) But he made up for his _bad eyesight with his local knowledge of the game in *Kathawali* and his skill in tying up kills at the right spot and finally making arrangements for beats and putting up *machans*. My father and old *Matru* were very good friends; a friendship which had developed over a long period. Mutual respect for each others capabilities, one as the expert tracker and the other keeping his nerves under stress and straight shooting.

I quite often accompanied *Matru* on his rounds to tie up buffalo baits for tiger. On this visit I had walked along with him, as he was tying a bait near a dry *nullah* bed where there was a big *tendu* tree, which seemed to have been cut down for no apparent reason. On enquiring as to why this tree had been cut and not the others- it was obviously the handy work of the villagers and not the contractor - *Matru* finally came out with the story after some time. This was the tree from which many' *Gora Sahibs'* had shot tigers in the past, before 1947, and as such, they cut it down as a symbol of protest. We all had a good laugh at that!

During my stay at *Khathawali,* I saw leopards on three different occasions. On the first occasion, during a *'ghoom'* in the forest in the morning we heard the *langoor* giving his alarm call to warn the jungle dwellers of the presence of a tiger or leopard. The alarm calls were coming from quite close by. So, along with *Matru* I went ahead to investigate. When we were about 50 yards from the monkeys, which continued to call, we were faced with a problem-how to approach further without making a sound? This seemed impossible as the

A Leopard jumped down from a nearby tree and disappeared in a flash.

ground was covered with dry *"sagwan"* leaves. We approached as silently as was possible in the circumstances. The *langoor* kept calling, yet there was nothing on the ground that we could see. Suddenly there was a loud crash about 10 yards on my left. A leopard which was perched on a tree eating a monkey, had jumped down, and disappeared out of view in a .flash between intervening trees.

On the second occasion when we were walking along a fire-lane in the block when suddenly I heard a rustle and the sound of a soft heavy animal landing about five paces behind me. It was a leopard. The leopard must have been sitting up on his tree- perch with the intention of launching a surprise attack on a suitable prey that frequented, this fire-line and would pass below him where he was perched. What a shock he must have got seeing a two legged animal passing from under his hideout and ambush site.

On yet another occasion, while we were returning to the *Dak bungalow,* on the spur of the moment, I decided to have a small beat next to a *nullah* about 500 yards away from where we were staying. Jungle fowl was plentiful in these shrub forests and late afternoons were ideal to flush them out.

I was standing next to a small canal which was dry at the time. This would give me a good chance to sight any jungle fowl which came over the open space. The beat had barely started when I picked up a movement from the comer of my eye. I turned and could hardly believe what I saw. A beautiful leopard was standing on the other side of the canal. It saw me and quickly bounded away in a flash. It was known that a leopard was in the area, but it had never turned up on several occasions when I had sat up for it with a bleating goat tied as bait and now we had surprised each other again!

At *Khathawli* another rare sight was a type of carnivorous plant which grew on the moist rocks near the dam on the lake. They were about six to eight inches high with flower petals like an open trap and honey drop like substance on them to attract their live prey. As soon as some unsuspecting insect sat on these open petals, it got stuck in the honeydew and the trap of petals closed on it. These closed petals after some time opened again with no trace of the insect! It had been eaten up by the plant. It was fascinating to watch this freak of nature at work.